Research Methods for Architecture

LAURENCE KING

Published in 2016 by
Laurence King Publishing Ltd
361–373 City Road
London EC1V 1LR
United Kingdom
T +44 20 7841 6900
F +44 20 7841 6910
enquiries@laurenceking.com
www.laurenceking.com

A catalogue record for this book is available
from the British Library.

ISBN: 978-1-78067-753-8

Book design: Matt Cox for Newman+Eastwood
Cover design: Alexandre Coco
Project editor: Gaynor Sermon

Printed in China

Research Methods for Architecture

for

Architecture

Ray Lucas

Laurence King Publishing

Contents

Introduction: What is architectural research?

As a discipline, architecture often struggles with the idea of research, leading to the question: What is research in architecture? The answer is not singular, of course, but as multifaceted as the discipline of architecture itself. This book is a handbook for research in architecture, considered to be a humanities discipline[1].

This need not sound intimidating, and it is appropriate as the process of conducting research has its foundation in asking a question. The ways in which you ask that question are important, and if you apply the most appropriate and rigorous methods, this will ensure that your answers represent an original contribution to knowledge.

This contribution to knowledge is the potential of research in architecture: to move on the established or overarching debate within the discipline, rather than replicating conventional knowledge and rehearsing arguments that have established positions and no clear resolution. In order for architecture to progress, we must continue to conduct research into its history as context and precedent; the social and cultural role of buildings; and the theory of what it means to build and dwell.

While technical and technological research is both crucial and valid, the purpose of this book is to examine the research methods appropriate to architectural humanities, developing the role of architecture as a discipline with an interest in the theory of spatial production, the social role of space, and the historical context within which we live.

Architecture is a notoriously broad activity. In this book I shall refer throughout to its status as a 'discipline' alongside geography, anthropology, history or chemistry. This is not to separate research from practice in an artificial manner, but rather to highlight the nature of architecture as a knowledge tradition in its own right.

Page 6: Kengo Kuma's Nezu
Museum, Tokyo.

Architecture is an ever-developing body of knowledge concerned with how we use space: how we dwell and occupy, establishing meaningful places and giving form to the world around us. How we build is informed by how we understand the world, and how we understand the world is framed by what we have built there.

The aim of this book is to assist the reader in producing research that is distinctively architectural in nature. The humanities do not refer solely to the topics within architecture with which I am concerned, but constitute a set of practices, a methodology, purpose and sensitivity to the world in which we live.

Vocabulary

Research
Research is the process by which you understand the world in a verifiable and consistent manner. That is not to say that research is not contested, but a transparency about the way that you conduct your research will strengthen your proposition. Research is typically conducted by the application of an existing model to a new set of circumstances, or by developing a new framework from empirical facts. Merely collating information is not enough to constitute research, however – the aim is to say something meaningful as a result of the data[2] gathered.

Practice
This is a term with multiple meanings, even within the scope and context of this book. Simply stated, practice is something that you *do*: an activity. You might describe conducting research, or producing a drawing, as a practice. Use of the term *practice* suggests that there is a wider context or supporting framework, be that the conventions of academic writing or the rules of orthographic drawing. Practice suggests a methodology, most often one that others also engage in.

Practice-based research
In recent decades, it has become clear that research can be produced more directly through a practice as well as through more conventional academic activities. Conducting research by simply *doing* architectural design is increasingly important to architecture, and represents an academic recognition of alternatives to the production and consumption of literature as ways of thinking. This is often expressed as the idea of 'thinking by doing'.

Discipline
A discipline is a field of expertise, an area of study, a discrete collection of practices, or all three. It is useful to think in terms of disciplines, as these can represent different professions or formalized viewpoints that do not adhere to a profession in the same way as architecture.

The inference in the term 'discipline' of a kind of strictness and codified way of operating is useful to think about, while not being completely true all of the time.

Cross-disciplinary

As soon as disciplines are established, of course, there comes a realization that they need to work with each other in order to achieve anything as complex as a building. In the commercial and professional practice of architecture, this will typically involve planners, engineers, surveyors and accountants, as well as clients. Research is similar, and architecture can learn from the work of environmental psychologists, urban designers, critical theorists and many other specialists. There are a number of models for cross-disciplinary working, with variations on the theme (trans-disciplinary, interdisciplinary, etc.) suggesting specific forms of collaboration. Fundamentally, disciplines rarely benefit from working in isolation, particularly when it comes to research: different perspectives allow you to think differently about places.

Theory

Typically, theory is understood as an overarching philosophy governing certain aspects of practice. The objective of theory is to establish something fundamental about how we act in the world, a result of considerable analysis and rationale. This might not be consciously acknowledged, and many theoretical constructs are mutually exclusive, denying the position of the other. What is important is that a theory offers a scaffold for discussion and informed debate.

Anthropology

A social science, anthropology is one of the most fruitful areas for cross-disciplinary collaboration with architecture. This remains an emerging field of collaboration, but the interest of anthropology in the various ways of being human, embedded firmly in a context, and examining the very nature of dwelling all contribute greatly to the understanding of architecture. The ethnographic method is also gaining favour alongside the intellectual rigour and understanding of alterity offered by the discipline.

History

The history of architecture has a great deal to teach contemporary practice. Offering more than just a chronology, there are themes and ideas that have consistently returned to the practice of architecture: the sublime and the beautiful, the Utopian alongside the functional, Classical models and romanticism. A great deal about architecture and the built environment can be learnt through methods of deconstruction and discourse/content analysis applied to architecture, drawings and writings. History provides prototypes, a catalogue of tried and tested responses to problems, subject to adaptation to new contexts and situations.

The etic and the emic

Linguist Kenneth Pike's[3] definition (further defined by anthropologists including Ward Goodenough and Marvin Harris[4]) of *etic* and *emic* research is useful at this stage. This is a crucial distinction when considering the role of architectural research as a scaffold for human activity, and represents two ways of approaching the study of how contemporary architecture operates in the world. The etic account is from the point of view of an observer who is outside the culture or activity in question, whereas the emic account is produced from within a culture.

This terminology is perhaps more useful than the conventional split between subjective and objective approaches, but more contemporary thinking is concerned with trying to break down dichotomies rather than reinforcing them. This idea is not used to express a preference, but rather to demonstrate a range of options. There are times when the etic is appropriate (outsider), and times when the emic is the most useful (insider). Rather than promote one perspective over another, this book aims to present contrasting and complementary approaches to the researcher in architecture to allow an informed choice to be made.

One fundamental question for your research will be where you place yourself with regards to the etic and the emic. Conventional models of understanding, founded on scientific or objective ambitions, will default to the etic in this regard. However, this is often taken to be aloof rather than methodologically pure. The benefits of such a stance are various: it might be easier to remain focused, for example – editing and abstracting irrelevant details that distract from a clearly communicated research question and your eventual findings. This complexity is often revealed by research in the emic mould. Fuller immersion in a culture avoids detachment from the facts on the ground, and a more immediate engagement with people and their lives. Much of the most successful research will move between these two positions, but there are benefits from a more singular focus.

Below left: Etic photograph of Namdaemun Market, Seoul, taken from a high viewpoint that distances the viewer, but grants a useful overview and depiction of the relationship between stalls, vendors, buyers and buildings.

Below right: Emic photograph of Namdaemun Market, Seoul, showing a view from inside the market. While more genuine, this approach can be more difficult to draw conclusions from.

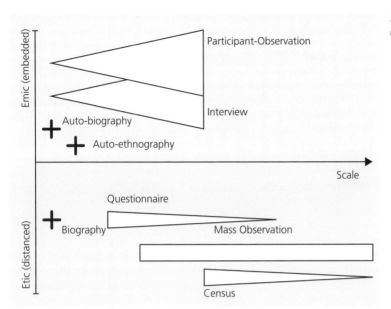

A diagram illustrating the etic and emic viewpoints.

Depth and focus

Multiple or divided research methodologies will split the researcher's attention and even allow inconsistencies to emerge. There is then the possibility for those very inconsistencies to become research questions in themselves, but the results are often muddied and difficult to act upon. A focused research methodology, immersed in a single approach, can often appear to be more thorough as there is greater opportunity for depth of engagement within the scope of a research project. While not allowing multiple facets of a problem to be engaged with, the narrow field allows the researcher to produce results with certainty, and that can be acted upon more easily.

Context, methodology and theory

There are a variety of combinations of context, method and theory. These are the fundamental building blocks of any research project, allowing you to determine which aspect is driving your work. This is a characterization of the research question itself. While not covering every permutation, it is fruitful to consider each focus as a potential starting point, with implications for the kind of findings you will be able to make.

Context led

Allowing the context to take the lead in your research process is one way of establishing the primary importance of the physical, social or historical setting. This can be used to determine a typical context, which

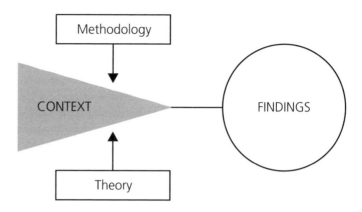

A diagram illustrating context-led research.

then provides an example of conditions found elsewhere. Examining a context as a case study of a *type* – particularly with reference to other circumstances following the same rules – allows a typology to be established: a repeating pattern.

The second form of context commonly discussed is the *unique*. This kind of contextual study seeks to understand what it is that sets a place apart as different and specific, rather than everyday.

The research context can be many things, of course: the career of a particular architect, a historical period, an established typology, a piece of architecture or a city. 'Context' is used to describe what the subject of research is, how it is located (where the idea of 'location' has an open meaning) and what its boundaries are.

An example of context-led research is given in Chapter 8 – a discussion of urban marketplaces in South Korea. This is a fascinating context, which is subjected to a number of methodologies and theories to make it more understandable.

A diagram illustrating methodology-led research.

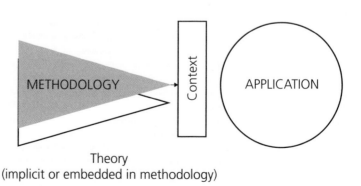

Methodology led

Beginning with an established methodology and applying this to a new context offers other possibilities. Methodological research places itself firmly within the parameters of this practice, often as a test case examining the applicability or relevance of a particular analytical model, or as a survey from which further research is made possible.

Knowledge of the method is crucial, and gives structure to the activities; from the ways in which data is to be collected, to the eventual analysis and presentation of results. A common criticism of this approach is that it is relatively procedural or completist and contributes little to our knowledge other than a sense of completeness. There is value in this thoroughness, however, and the temporality of studies undertaken must be taken into account – the context is a changing set of parameters, and a place studied according to a given method will yield different results, even a couple of years apart.

An example of this is also discussed later, in Chapter 11: the use of the mental mapping techniques of Peter Gould and Rodney White, and Kevin Lynch, in an unusual context – Jakarta, where the application of this method led to both comparable results and potential modifications of the original mapping.[5]

Theory led

Similar to beginning with a method, establishing a theory-led piece of research exists within a framework of understanding first, applied to a context by means of a methodology second. The theory-led process of research employs an established form of understanding in order to determine the deeper meaning. This is research that is critique, analysis or dialectically oriented. A number of different methodologies can be used.

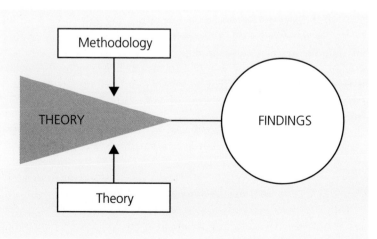

A diagram illustrating theory-led research.

Theory is a broad category, and the distinction between theory and method is not straightforward, given that many methods have a strong association with theoretical content. That said, the priority in theoretically focused studies is the critical nature of the engagement, where the methodology is descriptive. Theoretically led studies are most often cross-disciplinary, borrowing their theory from fields such as philosophy, social sciences or politics.

An example of this is given in Chapter 14: taking the work of philosopher Henri Bergson as a starting point for a drawing project, his theories on the importance of time and experienced duration to the creative act were explored in a manner similar to Bernard Tschumi's publication *The Manhattan Transcripts*, and with reference to my experience navigating Tokyo's complex and dense subway network.[6]

Thesis: antithesis: synthesis

The expression of dialectical thinking described by the triad of *thesis*, *antithesis* and *synthesis* is often said to have its root in readings of Hegel, and sometimes including *hypothesis* as a starting point.[7]

The term 'thesis' often denotes a long-form essay, a substantial piece of work establishing a theoretical agenda, but the word's origins lie in a more fundamental act of argumentation. This idea of discourse lies at the heart of a good piece of research, where positions are presented that are alternative to, supplementary to, or opposed to the author's own. The researcher must then prove their point, making a case for it.

Care must be taken not to set up a false argument where your position is deliberately selected to be ridiculous, absurd or indefensible. This leads to a sterile debate where the nuances of the case are unable to be discussed, and the synthesis ends up being a foregone conclusion.

Dialectical thinking is a process of first presenting a thesis or position, discussing its antithesis (an alternative related to this first position but differing from it substantially) and then elaborating a synthesis of these two positions by way of conclusion. It is a rigorous method of theoretical exploration that addresses more than one position and is honest about the disagreements while being able to say something concrete in conclusion.

Architectural history (not history of architecture)

History needs to be explored in a manner that analyses the historical record in service of the design of buildings rather than as a specialist subset of history. In simple terms, architectural history can and should serve the needs of architecture as a whole, responding to the role of designers in bringing historical precedent to bear on the present practice of architects as source material to be understood.

In elaborating architectural history, it might be helpful to consider the role of the prototype or precedent, as the evolution of design disciplines builds upon past models despite perceived ruptures and leaps such as the emergence of modernism. The early modern movement continued to refer to Classical architectures, stripping back ornamentation while aestheticizing industrially produced structures such as grain elevators and cruise liners – previously neglected quotidian design history replaced the dominant Classical versus Romantic paradigm, but precedent and history remained crucially important factors.

Architectural social sciences (not social science of architecture)

Architecture is constructed to serve the needs of people. This is a simple truism that opens up a much larger research question: How can we find out more about the engagement people actually have with buildings? The social sciences consider the contemporary context in detail, and encourage us to make fewer assumptions about the nature of our occupation of space. The simplest approach is to ask people, but this presents a number of problems. This is where social sciences can help, by offering a wide range of methodologies to help you find out more about the actual uses of space, and the importance of it in everyday life.

There is a danger in architecture and urban design of overly deterministic approaches to design: the accusations of social engineering raised against modernism are largely warranted and also the root of many of the failures of mass-housing schemes after World War II. Such developments attempted to tell people how to live rather than ask them how they would like to. Social sciences give us some access to how people actually live, what is important to them, and how something as fundamental as identity can be constructed through engagements with the built environment.

An architectural social science can offer an understanding of architecture as a set of practices. This affords the designer opportunities to adapt their approaches to meet the needs of clients and users, redrawing the processes of commissioning, designing and occupancy of buildings.

Architectural philosophy (not philosophy of architecture)

Architecture can be described as an understanding of the built environment. This is in addition to the conventional definition of architecture as a design discipline, but it is important to stake our claim to this territory that we have developed, through a variety of means, and a deep understanding of space and place – what it means to dwell and occupy. This is often discussed with reference to key figures in philosophy and critical theory. This is appropriate, of course, and using the theories of figures including (but not restricted to) Jacques Derrida, Gilles Deleuze, Walter Benjamin and Martin Heidegger all helps to frame our discussions.[8] The understanding of such theorists is, however, specific to understanding the implications of architecture. What does it mean to build?

Architecture demonstrates this understanding both through built projects and through engagement with theory. Often, the production of theory is conducted through explicitly architectural means. Postmodern movements and works demonstrate this most clearly, with architects such as Peter Eisenman, Bernard Tschumi, Steven Holl and John Hejduk all using the project, the house, the drawing as ways of exploring theoretical propositions. Such theory is designed to be read by visually literate architects, though: the reader needs to understand architectural representation in order to decode the programmatic element of Tschumi's scripting of extreme or unusual activities in space in his *Manhattan Transcripts*, or the way that Eisenman pushes the idea of purely architectural language and signification by simple rotation and duplication of grid and 'el' forms in his *House VI* and *House X* projects.[9] This pursuit of theory and philosophy can move into pragmatic explorations of the possibilities of architecture. For example, Tschumi's work on cross-, trans- and dis-programming of buildings instigated a wider discussion of the role an architect can have in determining the programme, opening up the brief to the design process more explicitly rather than being taken as a given.[10] This has further implications for the practice of architecture, seeing it not as a set of instructions from a client, but as a collaborative process with them. Similarly, Eisenman's formal investigations, conducted as an analysis of so-called *canonical* architecture, offered design processes that prefigured the contemporary move towards parametric design.[11]

The structure of this book

This book is divided into two parts. Part 1 looks at the fundamentals of conducting research, from defining the research question to conducting research in the field or library, and finally writing up and disseminating your work.

Chapter 1 begins with an exploration of the starting point for any piece of research: the research question. The way you frame the question is important, as it often forms the basis for the research. Key to this is defining the terminology used in the research. While this might appear at first to be a game of semantics, it is important to challenge assumptions that might be contained in even the most apparently innocent or obvious terms, such as 'space'. One example might be to ask which concept of space has informed this research. Is there an alternative to this conventional term that allows you to think about how people dwell and occupy in a more specific manner?

Once the terms of engagement have been carefully defined and referenced, the research question can be framed by asking, simply, 'What do I want to find out about the world?' This is, again, an apparently naive statement, but such questions are desirable in research, as they speak to more fundamental issues and assumptions that might be unpacked into something more rigorous.

Strongly associated with this is the question of how you find this out, as explored in Chapter 2. A number of research methods are available to architects, and each of these offer different ways of knowing – some of which might be more or less appropriate to your work, but that have an equal degree of rigour. This chapter looks at text-based and graphic research methodologies, as well as practice-based research, and emphasizes the importance of describing your working practice as part of the process of validating your work. It is not enough simply to express opinions.

It is important to understand that your research is strengthened by paying attention to the larger debates that frame your work. Chapter 3 covers how to assemble a literature review, from finding the relevant works in library databases, to the way in which such sources can be approached. Understanding different types of literature and how they each have a different role in research is crucial, particularly given the wide range of available sources, from peer-reviewed journals and the professional architectural press through to client websites and even personal blogs. Various institutions across the world, including the Royal Institute of British Architects in London and the Canadian Centre for Architecture in Montreal, as well as various university, local city and government archives, hold important primary source material, too, and this chapter includes advice on how to work with this.

The topic of cross-disciplinarity is addressed by Chapter 4. Access to what other fields of study have to offer is important, making their findings relevant to the production and understanding of architecture and the built environment. Collaborating with another discipline can be difficult, but the benefits of cross-disciplinary work greatly exceed the drawbacks, and this chapter includes advice on how to negotiate any issues that may arise.

Chapter 5 discusses fieldwork as a primary source of research data, and addresses how a field can be identified, from a national architectural style, to a particular city or even a plot of land or an architectural firm. Approaching a site involves an understanding of the place, and how people occupy it, and there are several strategies that can aid in this. Field research focuses on context, and prioritizing the messiness of real life produces research that is grounded in real life, but it can be difficult to draw clear conclusions from such work. Careful record-keeping, and use of sketchbooks and field notes, are crucial, therefore, and this chapter gives advice on the use of these.

Chapter 6 discusses interviews, a crucial way of gaining information from the wide range of stakeholders involved in architectural projects, from architects to clients and user groups. Interviewing techniques can vary, ranging from using carefully prepared questions, crafted to elicit a response within a certain range, to more open-ended conversations that take a more natural course. Advice on focus group sessions will also be included here, as an efficient way of presenting research findings to different groups of research participants.

Completing Part 1, Chapter 7 discusses writing up. Conventionally understood as the main element of disseminating or sharing research, writing is undeniably important, and crucial to this is a structured argument. It is important to see your writing from a reader's point of view so that you present information that is free of assumptions, and logically ordered. This chapter therefore offers practical ways to ensure that you achieve a rational structure, a clear narrative, and that your findings are presented in an orderly manner. This advice can be applied not only to the written word, but also to exhibition pieces, verbal presentations, drawing series and other forms of dissemination.

Part 2 consists of a series of case studies, presenting research projects with a focus on how each project was conducted and the way in which this influenced the outcome.

Chapter 8 discusses material culture studies, a branch of anthropology and archaeology concerned with the biographies of 'things' – those objects we come into contact with every day. This form of social enquiry offers a very useful way to engage with architecture. This chapter includes a review of examples from some of the important figures in the field today, including Arjun Appadurai, Ian Hodder and Victor Buchli, who all contribute to an understanding of the role everyday 'stuff' plays in our lives, and how this then offers ways in to the social nature of things.[12] The chapter is rounded off with my own examination of the material culture of the urban marketplace in Seoul.

Environmental psychology is another important field of research that has a great deal to offer architecture. This is addressed in Chapter 9 – in particular, the work done by James Gibson on alternative approaches to space, and the field of people-environment studies, where one of the largest fields of current research is into restorative environments, where richness of our built environment is said to contribute to health and wellbeing in a number of ways. This chapter also presents some of the findings and methodologies of 'Inflecting Spaces', a research project on the spatiality of the human voice, and how it operates as a determinant in public space.

Chapter 10 addresses the most established form of architectural research: the study of architectural history, the conventional Western bias of which is gradually being overcome by multiple, intertwining histories of architecture. This chapter presents and problematizes many of the approaches to architectural history, recasting the history of architecture as an engaging, evolving and live process rather than a neutral presentation of 'facts'.

Although the study of architectural history remains open to new approaches, you must maintain the rigour of good academic research with a combination of sources, from the contemporary to your own field visits as well as histories written by others. Alternative approaches from key figures in architectural history are discussed here – Manfredo Tafuri, Colin Rowe, Robin Evans, Joseph Rykwert and Nikolaus Pevsner.[13] It is important for architectural history to contribute something fresh to an understanding of the discipline. By way of example, this chapter includes a study of the architectural manifesto and its trajectory from polemic stance to position statement through the twentieth century as a way of exploring an alternative history of architecture.

The right to the city is an important concept, with its origins in the work of Henri Lefebvre, and underlines one of the most important disciplines contributing to architecture: an understanding of the politics of space and the implications of power relations in space. Chapter 11 discusses how buildings can be said to exert power over people, whether for a valid purpose or not.

There are ethical implications to our political engagements with space, so, rather than employ a single methodology, more politically engaged research can take advantage of a range of approaches. This chapter concludes with the work conducted by the 'Cultures of Legibility' research project, which looked at the city of Jakarta, Indonesia, and the everyday experience of people there.

There are a wide range of philosophical methods available to architecture, but – as an example – one has been selected to discuss this in more depth: phenomenology. This explores the fundamental idea of being. Chapter 12 explores two branches of this philosophy – the fundamental relationship between being and dwelling explored by Martin Heidegger, and the phenomenology of perception described by Maurice Merleau-Ponty.[14] This chapter also presents some of my own work on *sensory urbanism* and *sensory notation*, which was strongly influenced by phenomenology.

A methodology most closely associated with anthropology, ethnography is actually somewhat discipline-agnostic, and can be used by a wide range of academic fields. Chapter 13 discusses how it can contribute to architecture. Ethnography is a long-term and subjective study, where the researcher spends extended periods in the field to find out more about a given context. This is largely untapped as a form of research in architecture other than studies of practices and their working methods, but it has a great deal of potential in the study of urban design and post-occupancy studies in particular.[15]

Translating the findings of such research is challenging, so this chapter presents some ways of reading ethnographic studies, and how to use the literature generated, as well as exploring research into the anthropology of creative practice, based on my own work in the design studio environment, anthropological seminar, and at my drawing board.

Chapter 14 supports the idea that there can be an architectural research that uses the tools of architectural production as a means for describing, theorizing and explaining. The chapter goes on to present some of the problems and benefits of working with drawings, diagrams, maps and notations in your research. Practical issues such as the legibility of a diagram and the competence of readers to approach are addressed, along with some insights into research by way of drawing.

Further, this chapter makes explicit the possibilities for drawing, diagramming, notation, cartography and other graphic representations in the research process, bringing the results of research closer to the design process. My project 'Getting Lost in Tokyo', an exhibition consisting of diagrams, notations, drawings and paintings, is discussed as an example.

Concluding the book, Chapter 15 is a consideration of how professional architectural practice experiences different pressures from academia, although the need for research is just as strong. Indeed, much of the research produced in architecture is produced in practice, as practitioners are best placed to conduct grounded, practical investigations.

The investigation of a context remains part of the architectural discipline, too – meeting the needs of clients and users, understanding a building for reuse, or working with precedents in order to produce more engaging architectural spaces are all based on good research.

The connection between academic research and architectural practice is therefore becoming more common and formalized, as reflected in the increasing number of opportunities for practice-based and professional PhD research, which reduce the gap between research and practice. Although this book is primarily focused on the student experience of research, it is crucial to demonstrate how such work is utilized outside the academic context.

Conclusion

Rather than defining what lies inside or outside the realms of research in architecture, this book aims to discuss research as an expanded field of possibilities. Rather than there being a singular approach, it is clear that there are a great many valid and useful forms for architectural research to take. Architecture is, by its nature, a complex, multifaceted field of study, meaning that no single approach can tell you everything you need to know.

Researchers need not restrict themselves to a single paradigm of research, and most will be informed by a number of approaches. What is important to reiterate here is the need for openness and honesty about the process and framework of your research. Placing your work within the intellectual debates of the discipline is essential, too, for even if a work is highly original and represents a substantial move away from conventional models, it must say why and how it surpasses these established methods and analyses.

Architecture *can* be *many things:*

Architecture *can* be a political act: an expression of power relations.

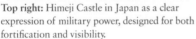

Top right: Himeji Castle in Japan as a clear expression of military power, designed for both fortification and visibility.
Architecture *can be* a political act: an expression of power relations.

Above: The Fushimi Inari Taisha shrine in Kyoto, Japan, the snaking path of torii gates working their way around a forested mountain, stopping for small roadside shrines and representing elements of the Shinto religion and philosophy of space.
Architecture *can be* a form of philosophy concerned with space and dwelling.

Right: Quingping Shichang Market in Guangzhou, China – where architecture is socially produced and maintained by way of practices, changing on a regular basis according to the needs of vendors.
Architecture *can be* produced and consumed as a set of social practices.

Bottom right: Ginkaku-ji, also known as the Silver Pavilion, in Kyoto, is maintained by Zen Buddhist monks, and includes carefully maintained geometric shapes in raked gravel as well as a strolling garden for contemplation.
Architecture *can be* a historical process and represents a culture of space.

Top: The view from the Rockefeller Center, New York City. This shows the diagrammatic nature of Manhattan, where land prices force buildings ever taller on their limited footprint.
Architecture *can be* an economic process which enables and marginalises.

Middle: Architects such as Frank Gehry often veer towards the spectacular with complex forms and expensive materials designed to seduce their clients and visitors. Other approaches include more subtle forms of beauty. The subtlety of Kengo Kuma's Nezu Museum is an example, with careful use of paper detailing on the interiors and a sensitivity to the pre-existing grounds and garden.
Architecture *can be* an art both sublime and spectacular.

Bottom left: The Turbine Hall at the Tate Modern in London. The hall frames large-scale art installations such as this work, titled *Embankment*, by Rachel Whiteread, 2005.
Architecture *can be* an ordered experience of and engagement with the world.

Bottom right: A building under construction in Kemang, Jakarta. This city is undergoing very rapid urbanization, with gated communities and malls being constructed at a high rate, alongside further development of the central business district.
Architecture *can be* produced and made, both in manufacture and consumption.

Chapter 1: Defining your research question

The research question – 'What do you want to find out?' – is both a crucial starting point for your research and an ongoing process of refinement.

Far from being a fixed title, you will typically revise your research question continually as your project develops. Research is not a simple progression from A to B to C, rather it proceeds as a series of parallel activities, looping back to revisit ideas.

What do you want to find out?

There are a number of ways of diagramming your research process. Popular approaches include the use of Gantt charts and mind mapping. While Gantt charts allow you to programme time spent on tasks in a relatively rational manner, they often fall foul of presumptions regarding the length of time some research tasks take, and the realities of thinking through a complex problem. Mental mapping, while popular in terms of generating clouds of relations and terms, can serve to disorganize thoughts rather than give them structure. Care needs to be taken with the manner of diagramming, as it reflects the structure underlying your research process.

The overall forward trajectory remains important, however, in structuring your research practice and, just as importantly, in how a reader will approach your work. A research question can be a specialized kind of title, and often fulfils this role within the text. This approach allows you to define your research as a practice, an ongoing enquiry led by your curiosity about an architectural issue. Your question might reference a specific theoretical framework, a kind of methodology,

Page 24: The Scottish Parliament
Building and gardens.

Right: Alternative diagrams
for establishing your research
question. This diagram shows
academic research as a series
of loops.

Bottom: Using a simple diagram
such as a timeline can throw
up interesting relationships
and correspondences between
developments in different parts
of the world. For example, noting
that a building such as Katsura
Imperial Villa in Kyoto, Japan,
dates from the same period as the
Italian Renaissance can form a
starting point.

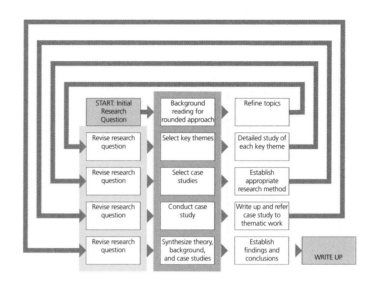

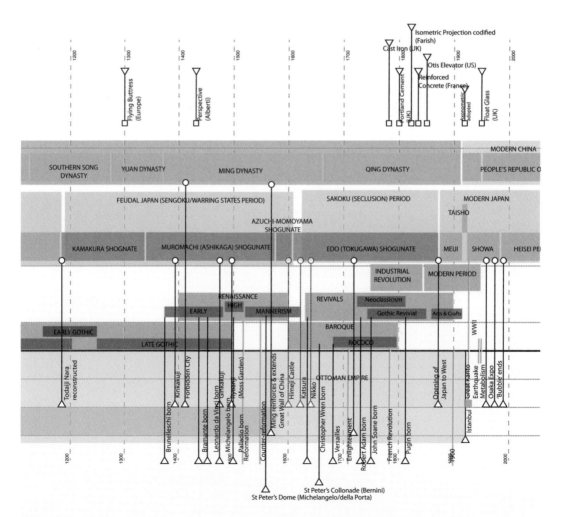

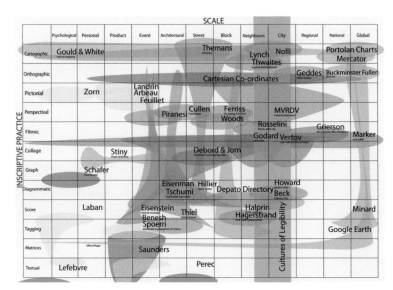

Left: Mapping against axes such as this diagram of alternative diagramming and notation practices in architecture can begin to identify common historical themes in representational strategies.

current developments in the field or some other reference point to give the reader a clue as to your own chosen context, theoretical framework and methodology.

The research question can be used in a number of ways. When publishing in academic and professional journals or proposing a conference paper, you might be asked to provide a short *abstract* of the research you are presenting. This abstract is a précis or summary of the research, focusing on the primary research question. This is more substantial than a summary, and focuses on what is unique about your work. The abstract is often used to print proceedings for larger conferences with parallel sessions, or at the head of a journal article, and is the audience's introduction to your work.

Writing an abstract requires discipline, since you have a very limited number of words to provide a full account of your research, and the aspect of it that you intend to present in your paper. It can indicate a larger project, showing that this has a broader appeal, but needs to convey the main points of your work:

Context: Where or when you are studying. The work of a particular architect or group of architects, or a specific methodology or technology can all be considered as the context of your work. Is the work a case study or a survey of a broader collection of works?

Theoretical framework: Which theories and writers have helped you to articulate your work? This can include theories you have taken issue with as well as those you agree with.

Methodology: How have you conducted the research? Fieldwork, interviews, statistical analysis? All are valid approaches, but outlining this from the start tells your reader a lot about what to expect in the end.

Each of these is dealt with elsewhere in this book, but it is important to learn to make your abstract both concise and accurate. As a student, you will most often be asked to produce this kind of writing as a more formal essay plan, in which case you should cover the following in addition to the above:

Structure: Break this down into the chapters and subheadings, with a paragraph for each, describing what you intend to say. Remembering the pattern of *introduction, development* and *conclusion* within each section of this is worthwhile; good essays often have this structure present at the macro, meso and micro scales.

Key texts: Slightly elaborated from the theoretical framework above, an essay plan requires you to give an indication of the bibliography you will draw upon, and for what purposes. Some texts are critical and theoretical, but others provide you with information and broad context. Each of these should be detailed here, stating which texts will be used for which purposes.

In practical terms, your research question has several versions – in the introduction and in the conclusion to a written work, and perhaps in some form in the title, even if this is implicit rather than presented as an actual question marked with a question mark. What is crucial is that your title gives some indication of the aims of the work. A fuller exploration of your research question should form part of the introduction. This allows you the space to develop the depth of your enquiry, exploring some of the implications and also explaining why you have chosen this approach instead of others that might also appear possible, or even obvious. Your job is to *defend* the piece of work you have embarked upon.

In examining a historical context, the work of an architectural firm, or the social networks activating a space, it is important to have clarity regarding what you would like to find out. Even when writing about your own design process and presenting it as practice-based research (see Chapters 14 and 15), you are challenged in writing a research question to say what your architecture is about. What is your agenda for the built environment and how are we expected to interpret your work?

From the outset, before you begin to find sources and assemble your findings, it is important to let your curiosity about the topic inform your research. Without this, your work will be an empty exercise lacking in interest, and simply displaying an ability to present the available data on a given topic. If you are clear about your aims, then you will have more control over the reception of your work. It is more likely to be assessed on the terms you set out, allowing you to determine the terms of the debate to some extent.

Defining your terms

Your question should include the terms of your engagement with the material, the context and the works of architecture in question. It is important, usually in your introduction, to 'unpack' the terminology you intend to use. In considering a word as a container of ideas, it is conceptually helpful to open this out, and, in an orderly manner, lay out the various constituent parts of the term, what its implications are, and how you intend to use it. Certain words might seem, at first glance, to be obvious and clear, but even the simplest language can be used in very specific ways.

An example relevant to architecture might be the use of the word 'space':
Space as geometry: The Cartesian coordinate system defines space according to three dimensions of X, Y and Z. This is an abstract definition of space, where every point in space has the same qualities as every other. This has its uses, but can also be problematic when discussing the experiential qualities of space.

Space as absence: Space can be understood as a negative quality, a lack of substance, bounded by walls, floor, ceiling or defined by some other kind of boundary. This has some implications for our representations of space and the ways in which architecture thinks about positive and negative space as a discipline.

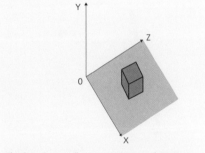

The Cartesian coordinate system's approach to space

Space as a container for activity: Space is where things happen. Often in the literature, the geometric abstraction of pure space is contrasted with place, where people have taken possession of a territory by virtue of their actions there. Defining terms in oppositions is one way to make your definition clearer, but does require you to establish a taxonomy or categorization. This systematization of your description can work like a map, giving potential new qualities, as Marc Augé identifies in his influential text *Non-Places: An Introduction to Supermodernity*[1]. In this text, Augé presents spaces that resist place-making, or that remain indeterminate deliberately.

Figure-ground representations using presence & absence

Space as socially produced: Philosophers and critical theorists including Henri Lefebvre and Michel Foucault investigate the idea that qualities of space are not so much physically determined as socially determined[2]. The same volume may be enclosed by a cathedral or a concert hall, but the activities that take place within each are substantially different.

Top: The conventional coordinates of mathematical space.

Above: A figure-ground diagram that uses concepts of positive and negative space.

The cave and the campfire: Architectural writer Reyner Banham presents two alternative discussions of space in his text *The Architecture of the Well-Tempered Environment*[3]. The cave is the bounded model of space,

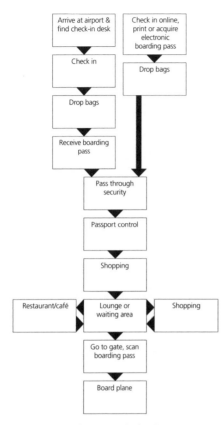

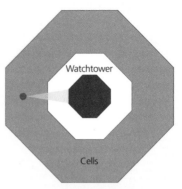

Prisoner's view – cannot see guard or other prisoners.

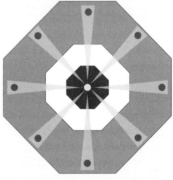

Guard's view – can see all prisoners while unseen.
Prisoners do not know if they are observed or not.

Non-place – space in the airport   Controlled space – Bentham's Panopticon

Above left: The model of the airport as a space that resists inhabitation.

Above right: Jeremy Bentham's Panopticon as a model of space that produces behavioural effects.

Below: Banham's notion of the cave and the campfire as spatial models.

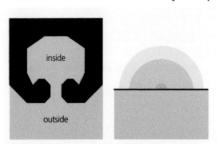

The cave and the campfire models from Banham

where a perimeter is clear and present, whereas the fire gives a relational, graduated notion of space as distance from a particular point and the implications of this.

Space and temporality: Often, the terms of space and time are opposed to one another, but they do not behave like a dichotomy: they are opposites, but in the sense of complementary ideas that operate in completely different ways. Otto Bollnow gives a particularly powerful account of this in his text *Human Space*, where the experiential is wrested from temporality and applied once again to our concept of space.[4] Indeed, many writers, including anthropologist Tim Ingold, argue that we cannot conceptualize human life out of context. It must be considered in an environment, since space is essential to being.[5]

Medium as an alternative to space: Other fundamental ideas of space come with the work of environmental psychologist James Gibson in *The Ecological Approach to Visual Perception*.[6] Gibson's model understands space as a medium, with varying viscosity and thickness, surfaces that mediate between one condition and another, and substances that are those hardened areas that remain impermeable. This model offers some frustrations to designers, but also helps them to consider atmospheres and materiality in novel ways.

We can see here that there are multiple ways to understand such a fundamental word as 'space', and that these definitions are sometimes mutually exclusive. Further elaboration in this case can be found in the work of Edward Casey, who conducted a comprehensive study of the concept in *The Fate of Place*, *Getting Back into Place* and *Representing Place*.[7] In some cases, the word is defined in opposition to another term, such as 'place', while it can also be given shape by attaching it to another concept such as 'geometric' or 'anthropological'. Given this multiplicity, it is therefore good academic practice to explain what your take is on the key terms of your study, for example by defining a period of history. Questions you may consider might be: What is the extent of the Renaissance? What are the limits of a geographically based study of London? How do you define sustainability?

In cases of real contention, one strategy is to actively exploit the tensions present within different definitions. This allows you to understand the flexibility possible within a word or concept so that it becomes a useful tool for thinking with.

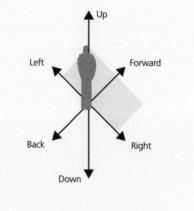

Embodied directions from Bollnow

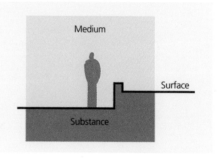

Top: Space oriented by the human body in terms of up, down, left, right, forward and back.

Above: Gibson's triad of Medium, Surface and Substance.

Framing a research question

Research often begins with a question. While this is a simple idea, it offers a great deal of flexibility to the researcher and expresses the fundamental character of the activity as grounded in a spirit of curiosity – what is it that you would like to find out in the first place?

The research question is different from an everyday query in a number of ways, of course, and must indicate several things about your research. It is worth remembering at this stage that it might not always come first, and that formulating a good research question is a process that you will benefit from taking some time over. Broadly speaking, questions can belong to a number of different categories:

The given question
You might be working to an assignment, and be given a question to respond to. This can often be seen as limiting, but it is also an opportunity as it takes many of the decisions out of your hands and

allows you to focus on providing an answer that is well worked out and innovative. There are as many 'answers' to a research question as there are researchers, even given precisely the same resources.

While a given question might be a substitute for your own research agenda in some cases, it is best practice to make the question your own, and to explore this further in your introduction. In straightforward and simple terms, tell the reader what your understanding of the given question is.

One way to work with a given essay question is to add your own subtitle, so that you are being specific about the aspect of the question you wish to tackle from the outset. This is one way of taking possession of the given question, and this degree of ownership will encourage you to give your position on the topic rather than simply attempt to present the bare facts of the matter. It is this differentiation that is often the distinction between good and bad research in the humanities. It is not enough to give facts, figures and information; your task as a researcher is to interpret this information as well – to take a position and argue for it. Even if your reader does not agree with you in the end, they will appreciate your efforts in constructing a coherent argument.

A gap in the literature

Many good examples of research are founded in a lack of material, identifying an area that has not received enough attention from the research community. This presents a significant problem immediately: where to source literature for your work. This approach requires some lateral thinking, finding analogous situations in other fields of study. You might, for example, decide that there is an absence of English-language literature on contemporary South Korean architecture. Your approach might be to look at regional architecture nearby, as well as the historical context, in order to establish why the area has not come to the attention of readers in your country. This can, in itself, generate a research question appropriate to your study of Korean architecture while also offering a framework for reference. Seoul and Tokyo are quite different cities, for example, but a comparison with a more familiar example like this would allow your readers to see both the correspondences and the differences.

You might take as an example the work of Arata Isozaki in defining *Japan-ness in Architecture*.[8] This text comes from a broader tradition of critical regionalism, establishing which elements of Japanese construction techniques and the underlying philosophy can be taken into contemporary conditions. This can be seen in the works of practitioners such as Kengo Kuma, who argues for the *Anti-Object* status of his architecture.[9] What is the equivalent for contemporary South Korean architecture? Your question could then be something like: How can Korean-ness in architecture be defined, and what is the influence of the Hanok house today?

Establishing this gap in our understanding is important to innovative research, but there are a number of potential pitfalls. One such trap is to give an account that has little or no referencing, claiming that this context is so unique, and the gap in the literature so large, as to present a vacuum for the researcher to occupy. This is damaging to research, which should try to refer to the broader literature. One reason for this is accessibility: the researcher's duty is to their reader, and it is a great help to the reader to place your thoughts within a wider academic context. This academic context will then also lend rigour to your study.

Taking issue with the existing literature

You might disagree strongly with the existing literature on a topic and seek to redress this situation with your own research. This often begins as a hunch, a sense of discomfort or dissatisfaction with what you are reading. This might occur for a number of reasons, such as disciplinary assumptions, the age of the texts you are considering, poor methodologies or political affiliations you take issue with. As an argumentative approach, this kind of research question places demands on the writer: you must state your case as clearly as possible, give a fair account of the works you disagree with, and understand that your role is to make a case to the reader, giving them enough information and a carefully enough constructed argument to persuade them of your version of events.

Above left and right: The Katsura Imperial Villa (or Katsura Detached Palace) in Kyoto, held up by Isozaki as a classic of Japanese architecture; and Kuma's Asakusa Culture Tourist Information Center in Tokyo, a new intervention that has been fully integrated into its downtown context.

Bottom left and right: Korean Hanok houses in Bukchon, Seoul – refurbished and new.

Above top and bottom: Two unconventional and adjacent images of the 'Duck' and the 'Decorated Shed': the Scottish Parliament Building, which attempts to display an attitude towards democracy with its cloister-like plan and display of Members' offices, compared to the Palace of Holyroodhouse, a royal residence, which has a straightforward plan and form that has been decorated with the trappings of a Scottish castle, but that serves no defensive purpose.

An example might be to look at an established classic in the field of architecture, such as Robert Venturi, Denise Scott Brown and Steven Izenour's *Learning from Las Vegas*.[10] This text has been well received and disseminated widely, but remains contentious in terms of its division of architectural works into 'Ducks' and 'Decorated Sheds' (*see also* Chapter 12, p.154). In taking issue with this approach, you might argue that it is overly reductive, offering a further series of categories for the taxonomy of image-based buildings. This might be associated closely with the research you have conducted in a particular city – for the sake of argument, Edinburgh. The collision of such a heritage-oriented city as Edinburgh and a very postmodern celebration of brash symbolism in architecture would offer you opportunities to discuss the limits of *Learning from Las Vegas*, or ways to supplement it in order to accommodate the kinds of buildings you have found.

There is a risk here of setting up an exaggeration of this kind of research – a weakened argument, whereby you establish a set of texts and opinions deliberately in order to tear them down, either because the issue you are arguing against is blindingly obvious, or because you are not representing the existing research in a fair manner. It is worth being mindful of this, as it can turn an otherwise rigorous piece of work into one that is mean-spirited and lacking in substance. Your aim should be to persuade people who might not begin reading your work as sympathetic to your position, rather than merely preaching to the already converted. You need to produce a usable survey, having an eye on how the material might be helpful to the reader.

A critical survey of the state of the art

A further category of research is the 'state of the art' survey, where the available literature on a topic is gathered together as a kind of extended literature review. A key question to ask here is: What are the criteria for selecting texts and examples? The criteria might be geographical, works by a particular firm of architects, or those that can be characterized by a style or period.

One of your first tasks is to define the criteria further, giving a detailed and justified account of the limits of your category. This allows for cross-comparability of the examples chosen – that they each have something in common with one another. This research question can be as simple as asking, 'What is the state of the art in...?'

A precedent study

Architecture is built upon the idea of precedents, and the close examination of earlier works. This approach to research seeks to understand the qualities of a piece of architecture, how it came about in terms of its design and commissioning, and how people used it once built. The wider implications and influence of a precedent are also important to consider. What ideas are inherent in this example and what kinds of new thinking in architecture were made possible after its construction? Simply put, what is the significance of this building or practice?

Your question is important as it reinforces your enquiry, and embeds the idea that you want to find something out. This is fundamental to research of any kind, and even where the results can be fairly certain, there are ways to discover more about the topic, interpret it in novel ways, or to suggest the wider importance and utility of your findings.

Exercises for developing a research question

Take the work of a contemporary architect you are interested in and construct a research question regarding their work.

Take a current news story with spatial or urban implications. It might be a new government policy or current events in another part of the world. Consider the implications that this story can have for architecture, what lessons might be learnt from it, and what theories might help you to understand it in more detail.

Now construct a 500-word abstract based on your take on the story, defining the research question and adapting this to form the title for the piece. Your abstract begins by stating the situation you are investigating, the details of the new policy, the responses it has had in the press, and so on. The next task is to consider the architectural implications of this. Some suggestions of the key literature are helpful, but this only needs a broad-brush approach at this stage. Keep in mind the implications your story has for the built environment generally, and architecture more specifically: this will form the key contribution made by your proposed research.

In writing the abstract, it is common practice to state what your research will do, how it will be conducted and what you expect to find out. It is good practice to use straightforward language to describe complex interactions wherever possible. Sentences can be written in the first person here:
'Through this research, I am seeking to understand...'
'This research shall establish that...'

Chapter 2: Defining your research methodology

Strongly associated with any type of research is the question of how you find something out. A number of research methods are available, and each of these offer different *ways of knowing* – some of which might be more or less appropriate to your research, but that are all equally valid.

It is important in any research project to be able to describe your working process as part of the validation of your work. It is not enough simply to express opinions, as your work cannot exist in a vacuum. This chapter presents a number of possible methodologies, to help ensure that you work in a way that will allow you to discover and discuss the relevant issues with authority and accuracy.

How can you find something out?

Simply stated, a research methodology is a way of finding something out about a topic – a set of practical and pragmatic activities that allow you to ask the relevant questions and achieve some robust conclusions. The most fundamental conventional division is between *qualitative* and *quantitative* research.

Qualitative research is, simply, the understanding of qualities. These are often understood to be subjective rather than absolute understandings, so that the categorization of facts becomes somewhat contested and based on individual or group perspectives. To many more accustomed to the hard sciences, qualitative research is uncertain and insufficiently accurate, but it has a role to play, particularly within the humanities-based study of architecture.

Quantitative research, by contrast, is measurable; most often associated with objectivity, this is work that seeks to establish irrefutable truths.

Quantitative research often involves large numbers of participants or significant data sets that can be analyzed for tendencies.

Rather than indulging in tribalism regarding which kind of research produces superior results, it is much more important to understand the needs of your project, and what is actually *knowable* about a given phenomenon. As we shall see later, the study of sensory perception in the built environment is a good example of a contested area. Different disciplines approach this topic in quite distinctive ways, but, as the foundation of much of human experience, it is a research topic in a wide range of qualitative and quantitatively oriented disciplines.

The degree of detail and complexity afforded by more personalized qualitative research methods might be appropriate to understanding a specific set of circumstances, while generalizable data about how most people see the world is achieved through a quantitative approach. This speaks to the aim of your work directly, once again posing the question of what it is that you would like to find out, but with the supplemental query – and to what level of detail?

This chapter will focus primarily on qualitative methods, given the focus of this book on architectural humanities. This does not exclude quantitative research, but in most cases, the more robust form of research for questions of history, theory, philosophy and the social aspects of architecture will be qualitative.

Text-based and graphic research methodologies

There are a great many kinds of research, so I have selected a number here that are useful to architectural researchers. The first grouping consists of text-based, conventional or traditional modes of research. These involve language-based investigations into the nature of a space, its occupation by people, or a set of practices. Architecture has the advantage of being a relatively methodology-agnostic, or neutral, research discipline, but this adds one more decision for the researcher: What methodology or methodologies are appropriate to my research question?

Ethnography
Ethnographic research (*see also* Chapter 13) is a form of enquiry closely associated with the social sciences, but one that is finding applicability far beyond this area. Ethnography is the practice of writing about another group of people. In anthropology, this would have followed the model of months or years spent living with people in another part of the world, engaging with their everyday life and talking to them about how they understand the world. By focusing on the ordinary, quotidian stuff of life, an ethnographer begins to understand some of the small things that indicate a more significant difference in world view or life-world. Ethnography is a longitudinal study: it is rarely possible to conduct

Typical Japanese homes in Kyoto, as discussed by Inge Daniels, present a different picture to the typical glossy images produced in the literature on minimalist modern Japanese dwellings.

an ethnography in less than a few months, and a study is enhanced by the length of time spent with people, as seasonal and annual events can be experienced, relationships with informants deepening over time. It is a deeply personal and exposing form of research methodology, and relies upon the openness of the researcher to a completely alternative view of the world and way of life: the ultimate aim is to understand some of the different ways in which it is possible to be human.

These are the concerns of anthropology and social science that, while aligned to architecture's interest in dwelling, are not quite the uses to which ethnography has been put within the discipline. One growing area of research has been the ethnography of architectural practice. Researchers such as Wendy Gunn, Albena Yaneva and Aina Landsverk Hagen have each spent time with architectural practices in order to investigate just how they operate on a day-to-day basis.[1]

These researchers have investigated creative practices including the use of model-making, the long life of discarded projects, the role of junior architects, and tele-working in offices in different locations, all of which have significant impacts on the ways in which architecture is practised. This serves to complicate and enrich the conventional picture of the 'individual genius' of the architect, seeing architectural practice instead as a complex set of social relations that are arguably much more interesting and useful to know about than the cliché often subscribed to. Ethnography offers further opportunities, and has long been used in urban anthropology, human geography and sociology as a way of finding out about the lives of people in different cities, districts and neighbourhoods. Again, this takes time and is a resource-heavy form of research, but it can reveal fascinating insights about a place and its inhabitants.

Inge Daniels gives a fascinating account of Japanese housing in her book *The Japanese House*.[2] Working with photographer Susan Andrews, Daniels moves beyond the concerns of coffee-table books on Japanese homes with their focus on minimalism and describes the flow of goods through gift-giving, the storage solutions key to Japanese homes, and the mixing of traditional and modern ideas of home and family (*see also* Chapter 13, p.168).

Rachel Black, in her account of Porta Palazzo market in Turin, Italy, took on a variety of roles assisting market traders in order to find out more about the practices bound up in this urban site.[3] The ethnography confronts the tensions between incomers and indigenous market traders regarding cultural identity, as well as the difficulties that shoppers face within the marketplace due to changing work patterns.

Another account of an urban marketplace is Theodore Bestor's *Tsukiji*, which considers the Tokyo fish market and its role not only within the city, but in Japan and East Asia as a whole, and also as a factor in global fishing practices.[4] By spending time at the market, Bestor gained access to the full range of its operation, from the spectacular and famous tuna auctions to the allocation of stall positions by lottery.

Ethnography is essentially conducted by mixed methods, but the key activity is to live in a context for an extended period of time, fully participating in life there. This *participant observation* is a key form of research that implicates the researcher in their own work: it is impossible to separate the researcher from their work when conforming to this model. Most attempts to erase the hand of the researcher are similarly fraught, but participant observation is rather more honest and open about the autobiographical aspect of research. Encounters of the everyday are written up as a kind of journal. These field notes are a key resource for the researcher, and daily entries are essential for recording observations as the period of research progresses. This can be supplemented by more formal interviews with key informants, who emerge as the process continues.

Ethnography is most often written up and supplemented by theoretical considerations once the period of fieldwork is completed. This can be written as a kind of prose, in a manner problematized by the famous collection *Writing Culture*, edited by James Clifford and George Marcus.[5] This book was influential in asking questions of the writing itself: the degree of scientific and detached narrative as opposed to the fully embedded and even poetic language of the encounters described. Each has a political implication, which is worth investigating and questioning: what is appropriate for your research will not necessarily be appropriate for another topic.

Marché Jean-Talon in Montreal, an example of the European model of a market transplanted to a North American context. Ethnographies are specific, but have an aim of producing generalizable principles.

Tsukiji Market's main circulation space, showing some of the secondary activities that enable the flow of goods around the market and out towards distribution and restaurants.

Critical discourse analysis

Critical discourse analysis is another method of critique – often found within cultural studies – that is appropriate to architecture. The operating assumption of this methodology is that every form of cultural production includes a series of reflections of the broader context within which it is produced. This means that the most apparently innocent forms of cultural production can actually tell you a great deal about the social context of their production. Critical discourse analysis seeks to analyze the hidden or less obvious aspects of a cultural phenomenon.

A good example here is cinema, which is examined not in terms of the director's intent, but rather the film's place within a wide range of cultural institutions, including studios, distributors, censorship boards and exhibitors, which all contribute to the public reception of such media. This takes the reception of the film out of the hand of the *auteur* to an extent. Such theories still hold a great deal of sway within the field, as they do in architecture, but the study of genre films (i.e. those not considered to be high art, such as romantic comedies, action films, horror, or science fiction and fantasy) often focuses upon this idea of their reception and reflection of a wider culture.

Critical discourse analysis allows a close reading of a set of works within a certain theoretical framework. This can include gendered readings of a discourse, revealing dominant attitudes towards gender issues. Other aspects can be considered in a similar manner. This theoretical framework is essential, as it informs the alternative reading that is pursued by the research. Without this, the research will lack focus.

Critical discourse analysis in architecture might, for example, consider questions of vernacular architecture. A version of this approach can be taken that expands upon the existing texts of Ronald William

Brunskill or Henry Glassie to use the architectures built within such continuous tradition and context as demonstrating the social relations and assumptions made by people on how to live.[6] In an odd way, Le Corbusier's dictum that 'A house is a machine for living in' informs this directly: Corbusier inverts critical discourse analysis as a design strategy, but there is a direct relationship between the forms of a dwelling and the kinds of living that are possible there.[7]

Dialectics

Dialectics is a philosophical method used to frame your research as a debate or discourse: presenting both sides of the argument in order to reason out a conclusion. This methodology requires the researcher to adopt both sides of a problem, and often assumes that the debate is somewhat polarized, with a *thesis* opposed by an *antithesis*, eventually resolved by *synthesis*, a logical conclusion that adopts some aspects of both arguments.

Thesis: A proposition, often written as a hypothesis in the tradition of a scientific problem, where an assumption is to be challenged. In architecture, your thesis might be to consider the veracity of a classic dictum such as Louis Sullivan's 'Form shall ever follow function'.[8]

Antithesis: Any proposition suggests its opposite according to this method. In the manner of an organized debate, you might be asked to argue for the position you are naturally disinclined towards. This is a rhetorical device that allows you to see the other side of an argument with the intention of strengthening your own position. Care must be taken not to establish an easily demolished thesis that falsely reinforces your position, as this is a relatively weak form of rhetoric.

Vernacular architecture from the Lake District in England. Materials and forms that are native to a particular area become essential elements of the architecture over time, and can be referenced in contemporary building.

Synthesis: Resolving the argument takes the form of a synthesis. This need not be an even-handed middle ground between the two positions outlined, but rather the logical conclusion of your presentation of both cases. Synthesis is also referred to as *overcoming* the problem, and this is perhaps a more useful term to represent the ways in which conclusions can be reached.

There are a number of variations on the dialectical method, but they usually proceed from the idea of presenting a *hypothesis*. Akin to the research question, the hypothesis is a proposition that you are seeking to understand or prove, one way or another. This initial hypothesis gives rise to an oppositional point of view: the *antithesis*, which, in this tripartite logic, must be given space to develop in order to balance the thesis that is being discussed. You might, through logical discussion, reject the antithesis, but must not do so offhand, but by reason and argument.

Both arguments need to be supported by evidence as well as argument, otherwise the result is an academic game that can go round in circles of logic rather than producing anything useful. The dialectical method is attractive for its logical procedure, but can be falsely assertive if you are not careful.

One flaw of dialectical thinking is that it can result in watered-down or even absurd outcomes; the process of balance allows only for moderate statements to be held, and also demands a resolution where many creative practices remain open-ended and in a kind of tension between one extreme and another without any clean and simple resolution. Other critiques of the method problematize the abstract nature of the dialectical process, which takes even the most ordinary and everyday problem into a realm of semantics and ideals. As such, facts on the ground become difficult to work with as they cannot be proven easily through such methods.

Dialectics of various sorts remain useful, however, when there is an established opposition to work with. Working with an established dichotomy allows you to reach a resolution by means of a synthesis, without having to artificially determine an absurd or patently untrue antithesis. In this respect, synthesis is not a melding or blending of the two poles, but a true resolution of the issues raised by the dichotomy.
Not every problem is so clearly polarized, however, and a complex network of possibilities can be ignored by careless uses of the dialectical method. The method is useful, though, for investigating situations that are contested actively, and for understanding some of the underlying politics behind everyday occurrences.

Reflective practitioners and practice-based research

The origins of this form of creative research lie in the fine arts, where a need was felt for research that respected the practices of the discipline concerned so that creative practice could be acknowledged as being an equivalent *knowledge tradition* to the conventional academic text. This field has advanced significantly since the 1990s, and is often formalized into Knowledge Transfer Partnerships where architecture is concerned. There remains a space for the practice of architecture itself to be a form of research in itself, however (see Chapter 15 for further discussion of this).

The idea of practice-based research raises the issue of what practice is, and how it can also be considered to be research: When is something practice alone, and when does it also contain a research component? One particularly influential text in this regard is Donald Schön's *The Reflective Practitioner: How Professionals Think in Action.*[9] This text argues for a model of practice whereby the practitioner is constantly critiquing their own actions, reflecting upon actions as they are taken and changing as appropriate. This loop of reflective practice, acting and thinking as a continuum, is one way of marking out the field of practice-based research.

It is often problematic to define practice without a research component as 'only' practice – suggesting that practice has less value than research. This is, of course, an unfortunate turn of phrase and nothing more, but the problem remains that practice-based research must work hard to establish itself as *both* practice and research.

One solution is to blur the boundaries between the two categories, which are convenient constructs, useful for thinking with rather than hard and solid concrete entities with unchanging boundaries. By recasting practice as a form of research, the critical content of the work is foregrounded. It is not enough for the production of architecture, be that through drawings, models, technologies or buildings, to be merely functional and in fulfilment of the brief. It must have value added in terms of an investigation that contributes to our knowledge of the discipline and the world at large.

It is this *unique contribution to knowledge*, most often mentioned with reference to PhD research, that sets out the research component of any work, however it is produced and communicated; you must still have a research question, a body of work within which it is situated (if not an actual literature, you can reference other works and practices in a similar manner). Practice-based research allows us to think differently about research, and to recognize the discipline on its own terms, to look beyond the text.

The set-up for a descriptive drawing workshop, gathering designers, architects, artists, anthropologists and a range of others. This was the 2009 'Designing Environments for Life' research project, held at the University of Strathclyde in Glasgow.

Intervention and provocation

One way of conducting practice-based research is by producing works that provoke a response. A pavilion or installation is the most practical way to construct such works in an architectural context, given the cost of an actual building. These offer a way of testing an idea, and later assessing the response to that experience. This can be a resource-intensive or expensive form of research, but art movements such as Fluxus would often intervene on the street with their 'happenings', challenging passers-by to engage with their absurd or strange activities, redefining the public and urban realm in the process.[10]

This research can be similar to post-occupancy evaluation and forms of environmental psychology, but it has a contextual aspect to it. Your hypothesis manifests as a physical form, an interactive environment, which might be a visual exhibition, an environment that can be explored or an aural phenomenon. You can record the interactions of people with this structure, conduct interviews and provoke reactions with the intervention.

Such exercises can result in quite violent reactions – hatred, disgust, discomfort, depending upon the research itself – and must be subject to thorough ethical clearance if contentious issues are to be addressed. The simple intervention into a space is a well-known artistic methodology, however, and the record of the intervention can be analyzed further after the event, so this kind of research relies on careful documentation and detailed analysis in order to be more than an interesting talking point for visitors to a museum or other public space.

Experimentation

While the experimental method is well established in the sciences, it has only occasionally been employed within architecture. In some ways, the conventional process of architectural design is not so dissimilar to the experimental method, whereby iterative progress is made in resolving a given problem or hypothesis.

By establishing an experimental method, some parameters need to be set: the activity and the means by which it will proceed. You might, for example, establish an activity for a number of participants to use a new form of CAD draughting. In order to assess the quality of this system, you need to have the same conditions and activity for each of your participants, as well as details of their prior CAD experience and general background. The experiment would be followed by an exit interview, and your research data would consist of the drawings produced, the record of the experiment you make and the responses to the exit interview.

Experimentation is a responsive form of research, as each experiment suggests the next step in your work. The results of an experiment can be unpredictable, but this is actually a primary benefit of the process – it allows you to design your next experiment to ask a more specific question, to interrogate a targeted aspect of the field you are discussing.

Validating your approach

Your research methodology should be outlined within your work openly and honestly, with a discussion of the aspects that were successful, as well as some notes on those elements that were less useful. This account of your research practice can include further references to validate your research methodology – even well-established research methods should be documented in this way so that your reader knows precisely *how* you came to know certain things.

This need not be exhaustive, but the notion of validation is similar to the process of your literature review. You need to place your research within an intellectual context, and discussing the methodological challenges you faced is one way of doing this. Architecture does not have a single method of research, and this is a great strength of the discipline, as it allows researchers to approach a wide variety of issues related to the built environment and our dwelling within it. Maintaining this multiplicity relies on clear statements of methodology that are honest about the limits of such methods.

Chapter 3: Building your literature review

Research does not occur in a vacuum; it is always strengthened by paying attention to the larger debates that frame your work. This chapter details some of the ways in which you can assemble a literature review, from finding the relevant works in archives and library databases, to the manner in which such sources can be approached.

A key consideration is the relative merits of sources, so a discussion on the types of literature and the contribution each one offers is important – particularly given the availability of sources, ranging from peer-reviewed journals to the professional architectural press, the websites of architectural firms or clients, and even personal blogs. Each of these has a role to play in research, and respecting the differences is the key to producing good work.

It is important, too, to assess the quality and utility of sources beyond the simple classification of journal paper or book chapter. You must assess the sources used by authors, their methodologies, and trace the subsequent impact of the literature, be that acceptance into canon or eventual contention and even rejection.

The use of architectural projects themselves will be a large part of this, of course. Treating such precedent studies as *literature* places them in a similar position to novels in literary and cultural studies, artworks in art history, or films in cinema – as texts that can be interpreted and interrogated. Key also is the use of archives and drawing collections. Various institutions across the world, including the Royal Institute of British Architects (RIBA) in London and the Canadian Centre for Architecture (CCA) in Montreal, as well as various university archives, hold important primary source material. Local city and government archives may also have useful material. This chapter includes advice on how to work with this – how to find relevant material, and what restrictions there might be on its use.

Page 46 Copenhagen University
Library, designed by Johan Daniel
Herholdt and completed in 1861.

In many senses, this chapter is about assembling a bibliography. Most
research will not consist of as grand a collection of literature as an actual
bibliography, but your compilation of a reference list is an essential part
of your research, and many experienced readers will actually look to
this part of a paper *before* reading the text.

Establishing your field

It is important in the first instance to identify the field you wish to study,
to establish its limits and collect, read and take notes on the titles relevant
to your work. This is, in many ways, akin to a detective story, as one text
will lead naturally to others and suggest new routes for your research to
take. Most pieces of research will begin from a genuine curiosity about
a topic, and there will be a starting point, a text that starts off your
exploration of the topic.

Where your field can be understood as a city or locality, there are
several approaches to take. Alternatively, your field might be the works
of a practice or an individual architect, in which case there are, again,
several ways to begin your work. Typologically based studies might,
for example, consider the history of housing, museums or department
stores. This suggests a specific way of finding sources including both
academic texts and, in some cases, legal frameworks and legislation.

There are, of course, a great many other possible fields for architectural
research, and this will be established in your research question. Your
task in establishing the field for your research is to explore all of the
relevant material related to that topic. Determining relevance is difficult
and contentious, even for experienced researchers, but it is an important
process, as just about any research topic will have a wealth of material
to inform it.

Informing the research is a key phrase here: selecting works that have
some bearing on the topic at hand will make for a stronger research
project overall, and will allow your reader to trace back your argument
with a high degree of precision. Sometimes a reader will be interested
in seeing what your writing does with a well-known text: Do you have
a new context to apply this literature to, or an innovative opinion of its
usefulness? At other times, a reader will be looking to your research to
provide a kind of annotated bibliography on the topic, providing them
with many routes to follow afterwards.

Finding relevant works

Your first port of call should be your institutional library, where
resources have been accumulated to support the research of students

and staff over a long period. Most academic libraries will also have a specialist librarian (some architecture schools still maintain a specialist library above and beyond this) who can help you to find the most useful material. If the library does not have the books you are looking for, then they should be able to order them in for you; indeed, where the stock is lacking, it is important to point this out, either to a member of academic staff, or to the librarians themselves.

Your library will run induction and guidance events, too, and it is important that you attend these as they are there to help you to get the most out of this valuable resource.

If you are writing for a specific assignment, then you will often have a reading list and required reading. It goes without saying that these texts have been selected to help you in a variety of ways: not merely replicating lecture material, but providing a wider academic context for your investigation. Look at the required readings in the light of your assignment and check any lists of recommended or further reading, too, as these will often provide assistance or clues for additional sources.

Most texts you read will have their own sources, and these can be consulted for further argument or information. Mining and drilling down into a text like this is useful for broadening your understanding of that text and taking the implications of it further; consulting the key sources they have used, for example, will give you a better understanding of their theoretical framework. Identifying that framework can then help you to find other texts that refer to the theories in question, and to make connections that the original text could not make – or even to critique and unpick its argument. Approaching a text as something that can be disassembled or unpicked before being reconstituted allows you more ways in to its argument, and more ways to work with it creatively as a researcher.

Searching the catalogue differs from one site to another, but this is often done through an electronic portal that allows you to search using broad terms, or much narrower and more specific terminology. When supplemented by searching other sources such as internet search engines or even large online bookstores, you can identify the books you would like to read.

It is advisable to move from broad searches towards narrow ones. Beginning with your net cast wide is a good way to ascertain how much material is available on a given topic before you begin to make decisions about which texts will be most relevant and helpful to your research. Learning to use your library's search engine takes a little time, but it is worth the investment since this will enable you to refine your searches quickly and find material that will broaden the scope of your research. Large national libraries such as the British Library can be consulted when you are using a large number of books that are difficult to source.

A library of deposit like this has a legal status, meaning that authors and publishers are required to send copies of their books there. The vastness of their holdings means that you need to be prepared in advance of a visit, much in the way of an archival research trip, as detailed below.

There is assistance in conducting searches from organizations such as JSTOR, which collates a large collection of historic journal articles across a wide range of disciplines. Narrowing your library searches can also be achieved by using databases. This means that your search does not include uses of key words such as 'architecture' by other disciplines such as computer science, where the term refers to the physical hardware used. Databases include the Avery Index to Architectural Periodicals, the RIBA British Architectural Library Catalogue and the Design and Applied Arts Index. These can be accessed through your institutional library.

A flowchart illustrating the steps involved in library research.

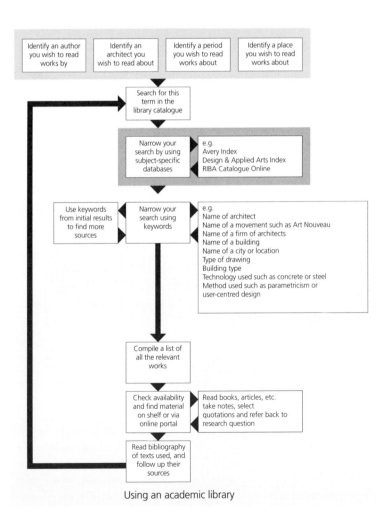

Using an academic library

Archival research

While most literature reviews will involve libraries and publications, relevant original material exists in a variety of archives, and provides an invaluable source for research. Archives are particularly important in architecture, as they will often hold and give access to original drawings alongside papers and correspondence. Material in archives is often unique, unpublished and unmediated by others, with the organization of an archive following the original order of its accession – an ordering principle that sometimes confuses researchers who are more accustomed to library classification.

Archives can be split into a number of distinctive categories:
Personal collections: A large number of archives are the collections of individuals who assembled them during their lifetime. These are often catalogued late in their career or after their death, once critical distance has allowed institutions to assess the worth of their contribution. These can be held either by a larger organization, such as a local county archive, or by a university archive, where the institution gains through the association at the same time as taking responsibility for cataloguing, giving access to and conserving the material.

Institutional archives: Several key public organizations, such as local government and city authorities, will hold archives as part of their governance procedures. Such archives form a kind of institutional memory or place-specific history of how decisions were made, the life of the city, and processes of planning and implementation.

Commercial archives: The largest architectural practices will be able to maintain their own archives as a way of enhancing their own institutional memory. This is relatively rare, and often ends with the collection being purchased or gifted to a larger archive.

It is important from the outset to identify the archives that will benefit your research. The original-order principle of archives means that material will sometimes be scattered across a number of institutions, but held in coherent collections that share a common provenance. Working with an archive initially requires the researcher to work with the catalogue and other finding aids, often accessible online. With the catalogue, you must search and select the material you are interested in seeing. Visiting an archive is not an exercise in rummaging through boxes, but a much more orderly activity that ensures material is left in both the condition and the place where you found it. Online finding aids will help a great deal, however, and often allow for metadata searches for key words associated with the collection.

You must then place a request with the archivists for the material you would like to see, and arrange an appointment for a visit. While most are completely open and free to access, you cannot simply wander in and expect to see material: preparation is crucial, as archivists need time to locate material or even to order it from an outstore. The archivists know their holdings well, and will be able to advise you on the time you ought to allocate to each record you wish to look at, as well as suggesting further material that might be of interest. Although you should certainly not assume that they will be doing your research for you, the key to working with archivists is to be specific about what you are interested in looking at; as with all things, the more specific your question, the more useful an answer you are likely to get. And if you are in any doubt about something, then ask.

You will be advised on the rules for each archive upon your arrival. Some allow digital photography, for example, whereas others do not. If this is going to be an important part of your research, then you must ask the archivists beforehand so that you are not left with too much material to look at in too short a space of time. The reasons for refusal can range from preservation (in which case you can order copies made by the archive for a fee) to copyright issues (where the archive holds the material but cannot give legal permission for copies to be made). There is often no room for negotiation once you arrive, so ask beforehand, as this may give the archivists time to arrange copying or discuss your project with the copyright holders.

Some material will be available online, which offers a very helpful facsimile if factors such as travel costs, fragility or conservation, for example, prevent the original from being used. Physical records are always preferable, though, as even the best digitization does not allow you to handle the material in the same way.

Each item will have a unique reference number, which includes the collection it belongs to. You will need this to order the material you wish to see, and you should keep a record of it throughout your notes and subsequent research, much in the same way as referencing a published text. This ensures that you are not only giving credit where it is due, associating your research with the archive that holds the material, but it also allows researchers to consult the same item in the future, to see if your reading of it holds up to scrutiny.

The practicalities of visiting an archive are covered in exhaustive detail by major national collections, so it remains for this chapter to discuss *why* it is important to visit them. First, even with topics that have a strong presence in the canon of architectural history and theory, there will be new ways to read it and approach it with each generation of researchers. History always has something different to tell us about the contemporary condition. Archives also hold material in its *most original* form. This might seem like a curious turn of phrase, but the notion of the *original* is a potential research project in its own right, so it is more accurate to say that the material is as close to origin as possible. This means that you can conduct research much closer to the

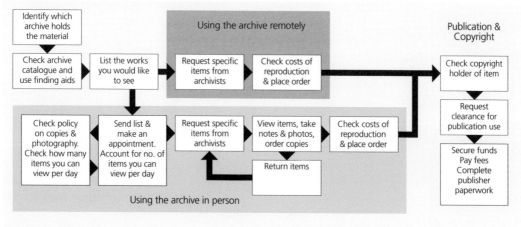

Using an archive

object of study, gaining access to the architectural process for example: what might have been, what was rejected, how one decision moved into the next. Archives allow you to see the broader constellation of interests of an individual as well: papers and idle thoughts that give access to the influences upon their work. Entire design processes can be present, absences can be as telling as the decisions of what is to be kept, and all of the actors and agents in a process can have some presence within the driest institutional record.

A flowchart illustrating the steps involved in archival research.

Interpreting material requires some position regarding the era of their production. It is easy to judge the past by the concerns and values of today, but historical figures can only ever respond to the circumstances they find themselves in, so a broad historical context can help to interpret the language you find in archival records.

Evaluating sources

A crucial part of your research is to evaluate the sources you are using. This should not lead to categorical decisions on inclusion, but should have an impact on how you intend to use the information presented. There is a broad spectrum of possible literature, from personal blogs through to peer-reviewed journal papers, all of which have their uses, but which must be approached on their own terms.

Peer-reviewed journals: These have been scrutinized by the writer's peers and offer the gold standard of research, but they can still be contentious and opinionated. The most up-to-date, validated research is available through journals such as *Architectural Theory Review*, *Architectural Research Quarterly*, the *RIBA Journal*, *Perspecta* and *Chora*. You may take issue with any sources, including journal papers, so long as your argument is validated by your research.

Edited collections: A book with contributions from a number of different authors and often subject to close scrutiny by the publisher as well as an academic editor, these are usually longer versions of peer-reviewed journal or conference papers by academics or academically oriented architects. As such, they are generally reliable sources. The thematic nature of such collections makes them particularly helpful, but remember to cite specific papers within such volumes rather than the entire collection.

Academic monographs: A book with a single author, these books are generally well researched and critically informed, with a wealth of sources and a strong editorial process. These can sometimes contain some unsubstantiated opinions, but so long as the potential contentiousness is taken into account, they can provide excellent sources for your work. Confusingly, such single-authored books are often referred to as 'monographs' in academia, but architecture has a specific category of architectural monographs that carries different connotations.

Architectural monographs: These texts are about a single architectural practice or architect, and, as noted above, are not to be confused with 'academic monographs', which are single-authored books. The access required to write them often means that books about a single architectural practice are rather uncritical, particularly when the architect is still alive. These are useful for background information, but are sometimes little more than published versions of the practice website. Where the authors are surveying the work of a historical architect or practice, they are likely to be a little more free to be critical.

Catalogues: Catalogues produced for major exhibitions are useful texts, and often contain essays by important critics, historians and theorists. Such books are produced by invitation, and often lack the critical edge of an academic monograph or edited collection: they will rarely challenge the subject at hand, or problematize them greatly, but they are often commissioned from a respected expert in the field and also include essays by the curators, so are valuable texts, with some of the best access to images.

Professional architectural press: This includes publications such as *Architects' Journal*, *Domus* and even *Architectural Design*. These are often opinion-based and lacking rigour, but they are generally useful, up-to-date sources – sometimes with some critical content – although not to be used in isolation.

Academic and experimental architectural press: A somewhat awkward category, but there has always been a range of experimental publications that blend architectural theory and criticism in different ways. Publications such as *Pamphlet Architecture*, MONU and *San Rocco* fall into this category, as well as earlier examples such as *Archigram*. These journals can be characterized by a somewhat heightened critical faculty, and flexibility about the means of expression. Where other academic disciplines might find these problematic, they remain some of the most interesting sources for architectural debate. Be mindful of the seductiveness of their arguments, however, as an underlying political agenda is often closely intertwined with the content.

Architectural firms' websites: These tend to present an overwhelmingly positive view of any work, but they can still be a useful source for discerning the architects' intent with a project. Remember, the jargon here can sometimes be impenetrable and designed to look impressive while saying little.

Clients' websites: These also present an overwhelmingly positive view of any work, but they can still be a useful source for some indication of how well a scheme responds to the brief, and further details about how a building is actually used.

Personal blogs: Unreliable and lacking rigour, you run the risk of going down a blind alley by relying on sources such as these. Check the author – are they a professional, an academic, a critic, a student? These sources can often lack the authority the writing suggests it has, so use them with caution. However, the benefits are that such sources are experimental spaces where influential writers can maintain a presence, or ongoing research projects can disseminate findings immediately.

Professional associations' websites: The websites of associations such as the RIBA, the CCA, Royal Town Planning Institute (RTPI), International Association for People-Environment Studies (IAPS) and many more can be strong sources for your research, but they are likely to have an institutional position that is worth being aware of. Ask if these are government-related organizations, with a regulatory role or other establishment/conservative position.

Works of art/fiction/film: You might have recourse to poetry, fiction, cinema or other unconventional sources. Where this is a print publication, you can cite it in the main bibliography, which does not need to differentiate between journals, books, websites, etc. Films should be cited with a separate filmography, and can be used as the subject of study, fragments of an idea that cannot be presented elsewhere, and so on. Artworks such as paintings and sculptures tend not to be cited in this way, but the name of the artist and the date of the object should be given in the text. Such sources should never be your sole source in an academic essay, but they can enrich an already well-referenced piece of writing. Architectural works are also dealt with in this way.

Generic internet resources: Generic websites such as Wikipedia are **not** reliable sources of information. They can be used to direct your initial research, but nothing from Wikipedia should be used without verification by another source: that source then takes priority as the more trustworthy. Such sources are useful to orient your initial thoughts, but absolutely must be followed up. Additionally, a completely anonymous source should not be used for an academic piece of work unless no other equivalent source exists. You must then justify your use of such a source in an explanatory footnote.

How to review a text

The process of actually reviewing a text is important, of course. This is fundamental to academic practice, and while each researcher will find their own way of doing this, there are some common starting points and issues to consider when conducting a literature review in the first place. One of the key things to remember here is that the literature is raw material for your research, and that you need not agree with it fully in order to use it in your research.

The author's notebook, showing note-taking practices.

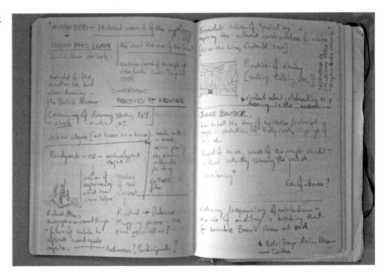

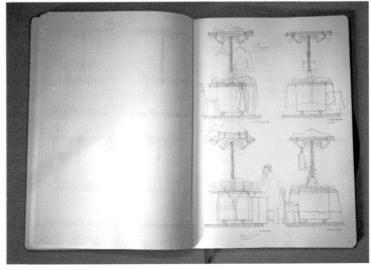

A close reading of the text is a starting point. It is helpful to take careful notes while reading, entering into a dialogue with the text with your own take on each book or article, noting the key arguments and how you relate these to your topic.

You will find your own way of doing this, but reviewing a text in a manner that reduces the distance between your reading of it and your writing of an essay or paper is advisable. It might feel artificial, but if you are making notes and transcribing quotations alongside your thoughts on what they mean to your research, you will be composing parts of your research and literature review as you read in a fairly immediate fashion. As shown [opposite], I work with paper notebooks as well as taking notes digitally. Circumstances and convenience often dictate this decision, and I have been moving more and more towards digital note-taking in recent years as tablet computers have become available. Note-taking in this context can be seen as a commentary on the text in question, picking out passages that are of particular importance and usefulness in elaborating a position. This develops as part of a network of readings and influences, so is always a draft, always contingent upon the next text you read or the next case study you work on.

This commentary needs to be edited in order to be made useful, but it provides raw material in the same manner as that created by the documentary film-maker Robert Flaherty, who, when working with the GPO Film Unit under John Grierson in the 1930s, would film substantially more footage than he required for the single film that had been commissioned.[1] Flaherty was able to edit one film from this before his money ran out, but producer Grierson was able to edit many, many more short films from this wealth of material. Your notebooks can, over time, become this rich a resource.

Remember to keep a record of your bibliographic references, too. This can be in the form of a text or spreadsheet document that builds towards your reference list, keeping careful track of the pages and chapters you wish to cite directly. Software such as *EndNote*, *Mendeley* and *Zotero* can also be helpful in compiling this. Recent developments include mobile and tablet apps such as *RefME*, which allow you to scan the barcode of a book in order to generate a bibliographic reference. (See Chapter 7 for further details on academic referencing.)

If kept with an eye to the future, your notebooks can be as precious a resource as your sketchbooks. The more careful you are in making notes, the more valuable your notebooks will be – providing you with something that you return to over the years beyond the immediate research work you are conducting.

Chapter 4: Cross-disciplinary working

It is becoming increasingly important to work across disciplines, giving your research access to what these other fields of study have to offer, and making their work relevant to architecture and the built environment.

Such cross-disciplinary work is not without its difficulties, of course. Collaborating with others is difficult in the first place, but when another discipline is introduced to the mix, subtle differences in language and working practices can cause problems. Most fundamentally, each academic and design discipline is interested in a different aspect of the human condition, and it is a function of cross-disciplinary work to respect these boundaries.

The benefits of cross-disciplinary work greatly exceed the drawbacks, though, and this chapter will give advice on how to negotiate this increasingly important area for new work, including suggestions for group working, collaborating with others in the same discipline, and maintaining individual identity within such projects. The key to this is often in documentation and accurate record-keeping of regular meetings, division of labour within groups, and a position towards collective responsibility once decisions have been reached.

Defining your discipline

Cross-disciplinary working is commonplace in academic research today, and is a crucial way to enrich research activity by opening up to the methods and theories of others who share an interest in a topic, but who investigate it in different ways, with an alternative focus. In short, there are some areas of expertise that are relevant to architectural research that you can benefit from introducing to your work.

Page 58 Collaborative drawing
'A Taxonomy of Lines' with
artist-anthropologist Jen
Clarke in Gallery Turnaround,
Sendai in July 2015. The
collaboration investigated the
nature of creativity through
the lines we make on paper as
a series of collaborative and
conversational drawings.

The first step in this is actually to understand your own discipline. You might be unfamiliar with calling each subject area or field of study a 'discipline', but the term is useful in describing the strengths and differences between academic practices, so I shall continue to use it and its derivations throughout this chapter. In this context, architecture can be understood as a distinctive discipline. It also belongs to a broad group of disciplines that can be referred to as the 'built environment disciplines'. This grouping would include architecture, urban design, planning, civil engineering and landscape – disciplines that share an interest in design interventions upon the world. Arguments can be made for other groupings, such as design disciplines or the arts; to an extent, such groupings have a historical character. Architecture was long considered to be the 'mother of the arts', for example, but has since become distanced from the fine and applied arts.

Thinking about disciplines can encourage you to think about the characteristics and interests of your own field. What are the boundaries between disciplines, and what is architecture in the first place?

The key to this within a research context is not to look for an absolute definition of what architecture is for each and every practitioner, but to consider what architecture means for you and your research team or practice. Every grouping will find their own definition, which will often consist of definitions for the following elements:

Context, field or scale of operation
Considering the field of study is important, as this is most often the significant area of overlap between disciplines. Concerns with the urban realm are shared by disciplines including sociology, anthropology, geography, political science, urban studies and development studies, each with something different to say about that context. Collaborations here demonstrate this common concern at the same time as contesting methodologies, be they surveys, statistics and data gathering, ethnography and other fieldwork, or statistical or literature-based approaches.

Methods and practices
Disciplines can also overlap their practices, and this happens most often within the profession, where an architect cannot act in isolation, but will often work under the guidance of planners and engineers, directed by a master plan from an urban designer, commissioning artists, interior designers and landscape architects to oversee specific parts of the work.

Results and outputs
The research outputs themselves can also be areas of overlap. Collaborating on planning guidance, research papers and exhibitions are all examples of the kind of work produced by architects in collaboration with others. The collaboration can be led very much by the expected result.

It is important not to overlay an agenda or manifesto on to this definition, as a disciplinary definition still needs to be an inclusive statement rather than one that only a narrow group of people can subscribe to.

This page and page 58: Examples from cross-disciplinary projects in a variety of contexts.

Identifying cross-disciplinary texts or partners

There are two key ways to begin working across disciplines: through the literature, and through collaboration. Both are beneficial, and carry limitations and restrictions as well. Once again, however, it is worth underlining that no single discipline is in possession of the complete picture, and that often the interests expressed by these alternative approaches will be fraught, and even mutually exclusive.

Working with the literature

In many ways, working with cross-disciplinary literature is a safer option, as the researcher is more in control of the process, selecting their approach and extracting what they choose from the material. There are some caveats, however. The primary concern is the difference in language and reference points between one discipline and another. Consider, for example, the use of language in your own discipline: the ways in which buildings and issues of architectural concern are used, the shorthand around certain architects and key texts. Such shortcuts exist in every discipline, and you may well need to do a great amount of background reading before you start.

A case in point is the perennial interest in film and architecture, which I share, but remain mindful of. Often, architectural students will blunder into dissertations on this attractive-sounding field due to shared enthusiasm for the medium. Film studies is, however, an established discipline in its own right, and has, in many respects, done much of the hard work for us in understanding cinema more critically. There are certain canonical theories such as montage, spectatorship, production design, semiotics, mise-en-scène, narrative, and gendered reading of film, all of which contribute to ongoing debates in film. Others from outside this discipline are also commonly cited: critical theorists (Walter Benjamin in cinema studies, as opposed to a preference for Theodor Adorno in the study of music[1]) are popular, alongside elements from literary theory, philosophy and cultural studies.

What is clear is that certain basic texts need to be approached in the first instance in order to contextualize the more targeted texts that speak to the topic you are interested in focusing upon. This means that the rather pleasurable prospect of comparing attitudes found in film to those found in architecture (presumably by watching a lot of films and deploying your existing knowledge of architecture) is complicated by the presence of a vast literature – a literature that you must, as a researcher, have some response to, even if you identify a gap in the literature. Further to this, a sub-discipline of film and architecture has emerged in recent decades.

This form of cross-disciplinarity is distinctive from collaborative working due to the grounds for the interaction: through books, journals and other texts as well as raw materials such as the films themselves. Opportunities for academic writing, design projects and film-making are all available as distinctive outputs of this activity, informed by the crossing of disciplines. Examinations of how film theory can inform architecture, through to the use of architectural styles and tropes in cinema, or making films as part of a case study or even design process, all have long-standing precedents.

Working collaboratively

Working directly with partners in other disciplines can be difficult in a number of ways, but offers a direct dialogue with experts from another field, who can respond more immediately to the questions you have, and who can interpret common concerns through their own disciplinary interests.

The first task is to find collaborators. While it is relatively easy to write to potential collaborators whom you have identified through web searches and contacted via email, this can have mixed results due to the level of interest such participants will have (they have no initial stake in the project, are too often treated like a resource with little of substance coming back to them, and they may simply be too busy to respond fully). When approaching people in this way, it is good practice to have something to offer them, be that a commitment to a jointly authored research paper, an ongoing series of events that you are organizing, or access to research and data that might be of interest to them. Without being mercenary about it, everybody in interdisciplinary research needs to gain something from the encounter. It need not be immediate or monetary, but some benefit needs to be forthcoming for each participant. One way to find more long-lasting collaborations is to attend research seminars, lectures, workshops, symposia and other events. Universities often have large numbers of these that are open to all, but that often have a very small audience in practice. Not every presentation will be relevant to you (or might not appear so at first), but there are often discussions after a seminar, followed by more social conversations over lunch. Once you have identified the field that you need to collaborate with, this is a good way of making initial contact, as the people there will be able to advise you whom to approach if they cannot assist themselves.

Professional events can offer similar kinds of networking opportunities, but it can be more difficult to obtain an invite to these. Polite perseverance, subscribing to mailing lists and seeking out relevant associations to join can be very effective ways of making yourself a part of any relevant ongoing discussions.

The way you conduct yourself is important too; don't wait for people to approach you, but be attentive and ask questions that you can back up with examples from your discipline that will probably be new to this audience. Participation is key in events such as this, and sitting quietly at the back of the seminar room will not open a discussion. Tailor your questions to your interest; use the discussion to gain some of the information you are looking for.

Once you have people to discuss your work with, maintain the contact: share some of your own work to let them know where you are coming from, and have a clear proposal that outlines your interest, your intent and what you would like help with.

The answers to your questions will be surprising, so keep your expectations in check and your enquiry open-ended. That way, you are truly collaborating rather than treating others as consultants or providers of validating information. Your collaborators will often suggest texts or ideas from their discipline that are foundational to how they consider problems and issues, and it is best practice to begin following these up, sharing some of your own influences and references so as to build a bond and a common language.

Finding common ground and a common language

In both of the above cases of cross-disciplinarity, there is no such thing as a stupid or naive question. Such questions are rather queries as to fundamental concerns that allow one discipline to understand another. This is part of the process of establishing some common ground, and understanding the contribution that one discipline has to make to a complex, knotted issue.

One of the best ways to begin is with the definition of key terminology. This is often advisable in any research project, but it is all the more important in studies that bridge disciplines, where the same word can mean different things. Several words have quite specific meanings in architecture, but carry quite different inflections in other contexts. This is sometimes due to the appropriation of words, changes of use, or their deployment as a particular style rather than as a theory.

'Modern' is a case in point. This one word has related but distinctive meanings in a variety of contexts. In architecture, 'modern' and its associated 'modernism' can broadly mean twentieth-century architecture (sometimes extended to include the Industrial Revolution), but some will narrow this to a set of styles characterized by the simplification or eradication of ornament. Architectural modernism is often described as a rupture from the iterative developments that preceded it, a consolidation of architecture as a discipline and an opening up of what was possible through building, which ran parallel to changes in society, culture and politics at the time.

Modernism is used differently as a term in other fields, however, and has distinctive features and interests. The association between modernism and political concepts of progress and globalization give the term very harmful associations in anthropology, for example. In the fine arts, modernism has characteristics of reflexivity: art that exposes the means of its production in some way, dissolving the illusionistic impulse. There is a democratization that comes with modernism: the commissioning processes and subject of artworks shifts away from old power bases and towards a mass culture, a mass media.

Practicalities of cross-disciplinary work

Working on research within a group requires organization, and this structure is all the more important when those working together are from a variety of different fields. There are areas of cross-disciplinary research that are particularly fraught, as long-standing misunderstandings between different areas of research can result in conflict. Some disciplines, for example, rely largely on qualitative data, others on quantitative. This fundamental distinction is not impossible to resolve, but unless ground rules are stated early on in any collaboration, issues can repeatedly emerge and eventually erode working relationships.

These tensions, be they because of cross-disciplinary misunderstandings or tensions of a more personal nature, often come up in research collaborations, so it is important to find ways to resolve these creatively.

Misunderstandings often arise in terms of the inherent politics of each discipline. Architecture is an interventionist discipline at heart. This runs counter to social disciplines such as anthropology and sociology, which have a bias towards observation rather than making any direct change to a context. This can cause friction, despite the shared concern with issues such as dwelling.

Tensions can be resolved in a number of ways, often most fruitfully by exploiting the situation and making it more apparent. Where there is a direct conflict, it can often be interesting to expose this fully and integrate the poles of a dispute into the research, its conduct and outcomes. This makes for rather unsatisfying conclusions, but does demonstrate the richness and contingency of everyday life, with all its complexities.

Resolving conflicts involves finding common ground, returning to the dissection of disciplinary and institutional terminology to begin with, followed by a restatement of the original aims of the research.

Where a research team has been formed from a variety of disciplines, common goals are important to establish, both in terms of the academic content of your work and the practicalities of the output in terms of research dissemination. It is important to discuss these outcomes as a group in the first case, and for every member of the group to both contribute and agree to the aims of the collective.

Position papers

If each participant constructs a position paper and presents this at the beginning of a collaborative project, they will make a clear statement of their interest and approach, opening up the potential for unexpected correspondences and shared interests, as well as highlighting any potential discord and heading it off as swiftly as possible.

Assigning roles and division of labour

One way of rationalizing the process is with clear divisions of tasks and labour, but this has some hidden pitfalls, particularly as any research process involves some dead ends and elements that cannot be pursued within the scope of the current project. When some members of a research team have spent time developing something that the consensus agrees to drop, this can lead to problems. So, while assigning roles can be a way of making use of the skills available within a team to best advantage, be aware that subdividing ownership of the research can be tricky when decisions have to be made about the direction of the work.

Maintaining identity

It is important, with this discussion of collectivity, to maintain the individual interests of research team members. Everyone must benefit from the collaboration, and this includes the disciplinary interests as well as the individuals. Collaborative working has great gains to be made, but also risks subsuming one set of interests under another. A good leadership structure is essential in balancing these interests.

Documentation and record-keeping

With even the most modest collaboration, documentation is incredibly important. Working with multiple versions of documents on a co-authored paper is one form of record-keeping; another is to keep minutes of meetings, noting the decisions that are made and the discussions that have been had. In many ways, the discussions are the real research output, not the papers, projects, data sets or exhibitions: a collaborative project lives on by opening new ways of approaching old problems.

Collective responsibility

A research group is a peer-to-peer relationship, not a consultation process. The team must be able to agree to a position and a direction – even where members of the group disagree with this during discussions. This is not a formula, of course, and group organization needs to be approached on a case-by-case basis, but transparency and clarity at all points of the process are essential for effective running of a collaborative project. Mutual respect is based on allowing each member of the group to express their position in turn, either in a paper or verbal presentation. An effective leader who is aware of, and responsible for, assembling the group also helps – so long as that leader facilitates rather than directs.

Collaboration: frameworks and practicalities

The way that we conduct collaboration relies to a great extent upon the number of collaborators. Working with a single colleague from another discipline allows for direct co-authoring of papers, whereas in a larger group, the responsibility for writing is shared equally between a number of authors.

Cross-disciplinary working often operates in one of several modes:
Architecture and…
> This relationship denotes an approach that takes architecture as a primary concern, but read through a different discipline, such as art or anthropology. *Architecture and* is a fairly procedural operation, simply bringing one discipline into contact with another in order to understand what they can bring to one another. One discipline is commonly dominant in this relationship, so you are attempting to learn more about architecture by applying the filters, rules, concerns and theories of another discipline. This is somewhat akin to the

operation of montage in cinema, famously described by the Russian film-maker Sergei Eisenstein with the formula: A+B=C, where this is also C>A+B.[2] Something extra is added by the relationship itself.

Architecture of...

Expressing the relationship in terms of an *architecture of* something else is subtly different from the above, and produces a more direct object of study. This is observing the architecture of something else, be that the architecture of social relations, the architecture of economic exchange, the architecture of luxury. This is the result of a concept expressed architecturally, so it is a case of finding a subject that has manifested itself through the built environment in order to understand just what influence it has had upon that built form.

Architecture with...

Working *with* another discipline is a more fully enmeshed form of collaboration, where one discipline is expressed much more through the methods and techniques of another. If architecture is presented *with* another discipline, then alternative ways of knowing and understanding are engaged with – ways of understanding the world are blended to the point where one discipline is read through another.

Architectural...

A further subtle shift is to consider *Architectural...*, where one might speak of architectural cinema, architectural geography, architectural choreography. Similar to working *with* another discipline, but going yet further, the aim here is to produce a fresh discipline that fuses disciplines together into a new sub-discipline or trans-disciplinary state. While respecting the usefulness of disciplinary boundaries, one way for knowledge to move on is to break down and reform such boundaries, whether with the creation of relevant sub-disciplines or indeed entire new areas of study, such as recent developments in urban studies or actor–network theory, which are beginning to take hold as stable disciplines, but have their origins in a complex layering and blending of older concerns. Sometimes it is necessary to look at things substantially differently, and this is one way of doing so.

Working across disciplines is encouraged professionally and within academia in the current climate. UK research councils, in line with those worldwide, stress the importance of working with different disciplines – not simply in the allied design disciplines of engineering, urban design and landscape, but also with geographers, social scientists and others. This is before even mentioning collaboration with non-expert user groups.

The dissemination of research output has enlarged from conventional lecture and exhibition formats to include Knowledge Transfer Partnerships. Designed primarily as collaborations between scientific research and business, these have slowly been adopted by architecture and offer opportunities for further work. Such partnerships are a crucial way of producing collaboration not only between fellow academics, but also between academics and practitioners (I hesitate to reinforce this rather false dichotomy, but there are elements of this differentiation that remain helpful and pragmatic).

The aims of KTP projects are to accelerate the adoption of findings from research, and to reduce the distance between theory and practice, but such partnerships also afford opportunities to move beyond supplying business with research and towards more fully integrated collaborations outside academia.

Conclusion

The philosopher Paul Ricoeur, in his account of language development, considers *metaphor* to be a powerful mechanism by which new meanings are introduced into language.[3] This process begins with a substitution, by saying that one thing is *akin to* or *like* another: analogy. This analogy is always made with reference to the original meaning and the original word, so that we are always aware of the comparison, always aware of the structure of the language. By introducing metaphors, however, Ricoeur talks of this substitution as being a way in which language can cope with ideas it has no language for, and that the metaphorical use of a word is, in effect, a completely new term. The potential of cross-disciplinary working is precisely this analogy or metaphor. By understanding one thing through another, you gain insights into your home discipline that allow you to move beyond well-practised patterns of thinking.

Further than this, as the practice of architecture changes – both professionally and academically – it is worth remembering that it has a relatively short life as a firm discipline: the term may belong to the Beaux-Arts tradition in the same way that master masons, carpenters and builders predate modernity.

Chapter 5: Conducting and documenting fieldwork

'Field' is a contentious term, discussed in great detail by disciplines such as anthropology or human geography, where the notion is problematized. Conducting fieldwork, however, is a primary source of research data, and it is often combined with other forms of research.

This chapter addresses how a field can be identified, from a national architectural style, to a particular city or a given site – be that a plot of land or an architectural firm. Approaching a site in practical terms involves an understanding of the place, and how people occupy it. There are several strategies that can aid in this, from understanding the history of the site to approaching local academics and practitioners.

Field research focuses on *context*, and prioritizing the messiness of everyday life produces research that is grounded in real life rather than abstracted and aloof, although the issue is that it is difficult to draw clear conclusions or recommendations from such findings, however well they represent reality. Good record-keeping and careful use of sketchbooks and field notes are an important part of field research. Other forms of recording and drawing are presented, too, with a brief overview of architectural photography, ways of logging your work and ensuring that the most important and useful images are captured. Other recording media such as sound recording and video also have their place, but must be carefully considered as research tools.

What is the field?

'Fieldwork' is a term commonly used to describe research associated with a particular site, place or location. This suggests that the 'field' is a discrete context, a unit of analysis that has a limit and boundary, however blurred that edge might be.[1]

For some academics, the field might be as large as a country – examining the architecture of Great Britain and Ireland, for example – all the way up to a continent or other commonly established limitation of extent. A smaller field is, of course, easier to deal with in detail. Defining a city or district as the field is one way to allow your research to say something comprehensive about a place. Deciding the extent of your field has other implications, too. By selecting a large field (often described as a *regional specialism* in other disciplines), where characteristics across a range of examples can be established, then comparative work is possible; families of typology, detail and construction could be catalogued in such a project. The smaller field allows for greater detail and more specific research – a fuller enquiry into a single example of architecture that can still refer to other places and representatives of that type – but it necessarily has a narrower focus.

Right and below: A series of drawings of the High Line in New York, combining plans with perspective drawings.

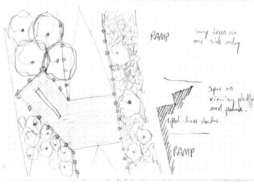

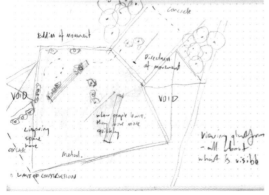

Other ways of conceptualizing the field also exist. One approach would be to consider the field as being the work of a particular architectural office – the practice of James Stirling or OMA, for example – looking at the key players, people who trained there and subsequently went off to establish their own practices, and other issues, all in the orbit of that important organization. This might be supplemented, in the case of a contemporary practice, with interviews or even ethnographic data on the work of that architectural practice.

A building type, such as an opera house, museum or housing, might also be considered as a field. Sometimes a temporal extent is included in this definition of the field, so that there are some limits to the scope of the study – a particular historical context might be that of the immediate past, the twentieth century or antiquity.

The most common definition of the field, however, is the most literal one: a more or less bounded space. Other uses of the word are helpful metaphors, and operate within the same mechanism: by defining your field in the introduction to your research, you are informing the reader of the broad limits of your study; what is included and what is not. This discussion of the extent needs to be justified and validated:

Below: Various department stores – from Paris, Dortmund and Tokyo – as examples of a type.

Why have you chosen this field?

Where and when have you chosen? Be as precise as you can be, and describe the conditions of any blurred or hard boundaries, along with the reasons for them.

What can be learnt from this context that can be applied elsewhere?

What alternative definitions have been rejected and why?

Above: The Rue Sainte-Catherine in Montreal, closed off from its usual purpose as a busy road and transformed into a public exhibition and display site.

Above: A pop-up restaurant in a Weimar courtyard, Germany.

Right top and bottom: The annual Sanja Matsuri ('Three Shrine') festival in Tokyo.

The applicability of such contextual research to other conditions is particularly important; otherwise your research can be accused of being self-referential, purely academic in the most pejorative sense of the word.

Choosing a field is one of the key decisions here, and requires a little more unpacking in order to ensure that your choice has a strong enough justification.

Type: Assess what this site gives you first as a *type*, as typical of a particular situation you are interested in exploring. What makes this site an exemplar? This speaks to the lessons that can transfer from this site to another.

Uniqueness: Second, consider what it was that attracted you to this site initially. What was your first encounter with the place, and how did you find the specific site within its broader setting? What makes this market, this dock, these backstreets both important and unique?

Accessibility: It is pragmatic to consider the accessibility of a field site. Do you need special permission to access the place you are interested in, and what challenges does this present? Is the site seasonal or better observed at one time of year? Does it vary across the months of the year and require multiple visits, or does it happen in a short space of time, like an Expo or the Olympic Games?

Informants: Are there residents or other people who live and work in an area who can be contacted to provide further information? Are there residents' associations or other local groups that can be contacted ahead of time?

Collaborators: These are similar to informants, but more likely to be local academics and researchers from different fields; you can also approach people from different disciplines, with their alternative perspectives and practices.

Preparing for fieldwork

Methodologically, there are a number of ways to engage with fieldwork. The direct contact with the field is what is important here: going to and spending time in the field will help you avoid second-hand observations or, worse, preconceptions and clichés. The actual methodologies are dealt with in Part 2, through the case studies presented there. The aim here is to consider what makes a fieldwork project unique, and the different forms of engagement with that site.

Visiting a site requires preparation ahead of the journey: gathering information about the social, political and historical context is a worthwhile exercise, as is gaining an awareness of the cultural landscape in film, literature and the fine arts. Coupling these with close examination of maps or sourcing information on the architectural scene, and any key contemporary and historical architects, are all ways to go prepared to your chosen field.

Even examples of cities in your own country can vary on these terms. For example, in the UK, London, Glasgow, Edinburgh, Manchester, Liverpool, Cardiff, Belfast, Birmingham and Newcastle each have their own architectural culture, from townhouses to terraces and tenements – different forms of housing related to their social histories, the key dates in the development of each city, the location relative to geographical features such as hills, river and coastline, and so on. Whatever field research you are doing, it is important to make yourself aware of this information ahead of the visit, so that you are better equipped to make the most of what is likely to be a significant investment of resources.

Further research can involve reading newspapers associated with the field, making yourself aware of the current politics of the place and what developments might be contentious or important to its citizens. If you are visiting an overseas location, it can be helpful to investigate the local architectural press, as this will assist your immediate engagement with the site, and give you some ideas for places to visit and people to speak with.

Documentation: field notes and sketchbooks

Documentation is crucial in fieldwork activities. One of the main activities is keeping careful records of what you do while in the field. Conventional anthropological practice involves field notes, conceived as a daily activity akin to keeping a diary. This regular activity can range from simply stating the times and places of your activities through to theorization on the fly, drawings to help you explore and understand your context graphically, and some correspondences you make with other areas you are familiar with.

A parallel activity more familiar to architecture is the sketchbook. This is an important discipline, and your drawings can include all architectural conventions: orthographic projections of plan, section and elevation; parallel projections (e.g. axonometric and isometric); perspective sketches, textural studies and portraits. Each of these provides a different set of information, and is valuable in its own right – but all the more so as a set of drawings that corroborate and enlarge upon one another. Sketches can be carried out *in situ*, but also *post situ* – from memory or from photographs. There is no hierarchy of one practice over another; it is more important to understand the benefits and drawbacks of each. (Drawing will be considered in more detail in Chapter 14.)

Your field notes and sketchbooks are highly personal in nature and must be distilled in order to be communicable to a reader outside your immediate research group. This might mean rewriting or redrawing as appropriate, but your notes remain an extremely useful first draft and subsequent, recurring source for your research. The power lies in the immediacy of a notebook. It is portable, requires the simplest technologies of pen, pencil, rulers and tape, and is flexible – elements can be pasted in, multiple media can be used, and you can shift seamlessly from drawing to writing to collage and back again.

Collecting material culture, particularly paper objects, can be helpful. Newspapers again are helpful, but area guides, tourist documentation and other leaflets will all assist in processing what you have observed. Take care not to take such sources at face value as they often have a vested interest or bias to them, but such ephemera can be helpful as thinking tools while you are in the field, and as mementos after the fact.

Key to successful use of each of these activities is organization. Make sure that everything is dated, with the location noted. You may think at the time that you will remember, but you should expect to be working with fieldwork data for some time after your trip, and some of the finer details may escape you if you do not keep records.

Recording media: photography, video and audio

Photography, video and audio are, of course, extremely valuable research tools, but they must be approached with care and attention. Remember at all times to be sensitive to people's desire to be photographed and recorded: some people are okay with this, but others will not wish to be captured in this way, for whatever reason. Make yourself aware of your institution's ethics guidelines, and let the context guide you. People are often willing to be photographed in public spaces so long as you are quick and unintrusive. For certain types of photographs – close portraits, or shots of the interiors of private buildings, for example – you need permission, and you must respect this in order to keep your research ethically sound.

Architectural photography in its conventional mode leaves itself open to many criticisms, mostly related to the perfect image presented, evacuated of any trace of human occupation.[2] This is, of course, only part of the story, but spending time learning the capabilities of your camera yields significant benefits in your fieldwork. If you are borrowing cameras from your academic institution or architectural practice, take the time to test them out at home first. Practical issues, such as the length of time your battery can be expected to last, through to the technicalities of different lenses, are all worth becoming familiar with. You will want to be able to react to the context you are in. Sometimes this will require an ability to shoot quickly; other times you will be able to get that slowly composed, perfectly framed shot of a building or context.

Photography equipment for fieldwork, including a good quality digital camera with video recording functions, alternative lenses for zoom, macro and wide angles, spare battery, cleaning equipment and mobile phone as backup. A tripod is also essential for certain shots, such as night shooting.

Remember basic equipment – a tripod can work wonders for your shots, although not every field will lend itself to it. Being able to open the aperture up wide (represented by a lower f number, such as f1.8) allows for clearer and sharper shots in challenging light conditions, but also gives a shallow depth of field. This can be attractive as the point of focus can be used to select the part of the field of vision you are interested in, but the aim of research shots is often to capture as much as possible, so a smaller aperture might be better.[3]

Be aware of lighting conditions and your shooting position, too. If you are looking to do a lot of up-close street photography, then a wide-angle lens will help. With the focal length of lenses measured in millimetres, a lower number gives a wider angle, taking in more of the scene at once.

(Relative to the 'normal' – most often in 35mm photography, a lens of 50mm is considered to be the normal lens, a kind of baseline generated by the size of the sensor. Cameras tend to list the 35mm equivalent values nowadays, with the proliferation of different standards in digital photography.) Very wide-angle lenses begin to distort, of course, and should be avoided unless there is a particular creative requirement for this kind of photography.

Zoom lenses offer greater opportunities for shooting at a distance, and can be helpful in some aspects of architectural photography for selecting details. Such lenses can be figuratively distancing (as well as actually producing this distance between the photographer and their subject), so should also be used with some caution.

Some cameras will offer a wide-range fixed lens, which shoots from wide angle to zoom. While practical and often cheaper, such cameras might not produce as high quality an image as a compact system or DSLR camera. In this case, it is worth considering the uses you intend to put your photographs to: if you are going to exhibit or publish the images, then quality is important and needs to be attended to, otherwise a relatively cheap camera (even a mobile phone camera) can produce very good results in the right hands.

Video is also very useful in recording a fieldwork context. The usability of video for further research output is somewhat limited, however, so remember that photography fits better with most conventional modes of dissemination, such as a lecture or written paper. Video allows you to capture the ambience of a scene as it unfolds – the ways in which people use a place. The difficulties of photography are compounded by video, however, as it is a technology that often places an opposition between the observer and the observed fairly immediately. People can be nervous in front of cameras, too – video cameras much more than stills.

Again, knowing your equipment is important, so that you can respond to the context quickly. Getting the most out of your fieldwork recording relies much more on your ability to use the equipment than on the quality that it can capture. Practise your fieldwork methodologies at home, review the footage and think carefully about what it gives you in terms of your research.

The focus, framing and movement of the camera are all important factors to consider here. Watch documentary films critically to see examples of how different shot types are used, and test these yourself. A common failing of footage shot in the field is the tendency towards over-complication. Good results can come from the simplicity of setting the camera on a tripod and letting it run – just point it in the relevant direction and leave it alone.

If you are looking to use footage as part of your research dissemination and output, you will need to edit it. This process can inform the shots you take out in the field, as it is often uncomfortable to watch a scene on film longer than 30 to 210 seconds long – unless you are a top art-house director, or have footage that holds the attention fully with events happening and developing constantly. Shoot more footage than you need, as this gives you flexibility when editing, and remember to get some establishing shots that will help you to understand the context before getting to the heart of your research.

Audio equipment for fieldwork, including digital audio recorder, wind jammer, remote, spare batteries, earphones, alternative specialist microphones such as binaural microphones, and a tripod for stability.

The third recording medium is sound. This is worth paying attention to with reference to the above notes on video, but can also be decoupled from the image in order to produce a soundscape recording. There are certain basic things to remember when making sound recordings. Most of these are the result of microphones behaving differently to the human ear: they simply pick up sounds unselectively, whereas our experience of hearing has several filters and controls to allow us to subconsciously attend to the most important sounds. For external recordings, make sure you have a wind baffle or wind sock to cover the microphone, otherwise you will pick up even the mildest of wind as a distracting whooshing noise. Another technicality is checking the levels of the recording to make sure it is not peaking with particularly high-pitched sounds. Consult the manual for your audio recorder to find out how to do this for your model, as this will give you much clearer and more usable recordings. Obviously, audio recorders are useful for interviews as well as environmental recordings, and a dedicated recorder is often superior to a mobile phone application. At short notice or in an emergency, however, a phone is a good backup.

For environmental recordings, pay attention to your own clothing: squeaky shoes and swishing jackets or clacking bangles will be picked up by the microphone, announcing your presence within the space rather obviously. If this is not your intention (and this will rarely be the case), then be mindful of the amount of noise you make.

Think about audio recording in a similar manner to video. Do you take a static position or do you move? Do you follow a subject or allow the world to move past you? Finally, with recording, think carefully about the audio equipment you wish to use. Solid-state digital recorders are the norm nowadays, as there is no in-recorder equipment. This is an advantage over most video and stills cameras, where the equipment can have a fair amount of noise inherent to its operation. The microphone is hugely important and, as with camera lenses, there are a variety of types to deal with different tasks. Condenser and omni-directional microphones are the most ubiquitous, and tend to have a number of microphone heads in a single body. This gives them a flexibility that is helpful in most situations. Condensors are more targeted microphones, while omni-directional microphones pick up a wider range of sounds. Specialized circumstances might make a shotgun microphone appropriate, in order to capture distant sounds; binaural microphones, which are worn in the ears like earphones, capture environmental recordings of some accuracy when played back through headphones.

If you are using an audio recorder in conjunction with video recording in order to improve the quality, remember to make a registration sound such as clapping your hands in order to synchronize the tracks. Also, if you are recording an interior and intend to edit clips (such as in an interview to be used in an exhibition or film), record a clip of the ambience of the place to use in place of absolute silence; subtle cues can be picked up when listening that makes an artificial silence stand out.

Analysis of fieldwork

It might seem that fieldwork is largely conducted in the field, but this is only a part of what happens: the bulk of the time spent on field research is often after the fact, *post situ*, working through the field notes, sketchbooks, drawings, photographs and recordings.

As noted above, editing is one important process in making any of this material digestible for an outside audience, but more than that, it is an ordering and structuring process that helps you to make sense of it yourself. Sometimes the point of editing is to find the underlying narrative – long before you would even think of showing it to an audience.

Fieldwork is only part of the story, of course, and requires close analysis with reference to the theoretical concerns that emerge. Treat the data much as you would a text from your literature review: give it equal status – you have spent time gathering this data for yourself, so you can consider it to be reliable and consistent. This does not mean to say that you can extrapolate infinitely from your account, of course. It is reliable within its own boundaries – of that place and time, as understood through your observational methodologies. It is the description of your methodology that lends credence and rigour to your observations.

Use small episodes to build larger ideas: some incidents will contain within them much of the complexity of a space, and a well-written description of these key incidents should be your first task upon returning from field research. This should be based on your field notes and other evidence, but the point of fieldwork is to give you descriptive material. This can then be understood in different ways, according to the interest that you are bringing to the context, or – if you are approaching things from the other direction – should generate enough questions to suggest the appropriate direction for your reading.

Analysis is a process of understanding and extracting the relevant information from a mass of data. While it can be overwhelming, examining short episodes is one good way to begin building up that picture into an engaging and useful narrative. It is then open to you as a researcher to make those observations work for you in the production of some larger ideas and theories of your own – all based on the reality of what you observed in the field.

Chapter 6: Conducting interviews

Interviews are a crucial way of gaining research information from the wide range of people involved in architectural projects, from the architects to clients and user groups.

Interviewing techniques take several forms. Some involve prepared questions, carefully crafted to elicit a response within a certain range, whereas other interviews can be more open-ended in order to allow the conversation to take a more natural course. Focus group sessions offer an efficient way of presenting research questions and findings to different groups of research participants and peer groups.

Conducting interviews requires some care with regards to research ethics. The power relations inherent in any discourse must be carefully considered to ensure that research is conducted in a fair manner, not risking the position of the interviewee at all. This might mean anonymizing interviewees, retaining any sensitive data and taking care over dissemination. This chapter takes you through these issues, discusses how to resolve them, and how to prepare a research proposal for consideration by an ethics committee where appropriate.

Conducting communications in other ways – for example, through phone interviews or correspondence – requires a professional tone, clear communication skills and an honest statement of your intent. Such structured and unstructured encounters with others can be the most difficult forms of research to negotiate, particularly as the responses given can present difficulties.

Modern alternatives allow for innovative forms of crowd-sourcing information. This chapter frames the use of social media such as Twitter, Facebook, LinkedIn and online survey platforms as integral parts of the interview process, and subject to many of the same ethical concerns.

The analysis of interviews is essential for translating data into research, and there are several ways in which this can be done. Where an individual interviewee is a key stakeholder in a project under examination, for example, their account of a design or process can be very valuable, if informed largely by opinion. This needs to be processed in a different way to data deriving from large numbers of questionnaires, where key terminology might be identified, or various means of aggregating opinions used to draw conclusions. This chapter shall suggest ways to construct questionnaires and interviews to help researchers to gain the most from such activities.

Who should you interview?

It is important, of course, to ensure that you are interviewing the correct people for your chosen research project. This will not always be a principal architect or designer, but instead may include building users, clients, local building authorities or planning officers. Each of these groups necessitates a different approach to interviewing, and must respond to their capacity to answer your questions.

Each individual can contribute something distinctive to an account of a project you would like to know more about. The designer, for example, can speak about the process of establishing the details of the scheme, the factors that generated the form, the relationship with client and context, as well as considering the theoretical underpinnings of that process. Architects will vary as much as any other group of individuals, so it is worth bearing in mind that they will tend to present their work in as positive a light as possible: every group, every individual will have a vested interest in the account that they give. This bias is not problematic in itself; it is merely a factor that you must be fully aware of when presenting the interview in your essay, paper or other dissemination.

Assessing the candidacy of interviewees is important. There are aspects of a building's ongoing operation that an architect cannot, for example, speak to: this might be the domain of other professionals such as engineers or project managers, or might be something that only long-term users can reveal, so make sure that you consult the most useful individuals. The availability of interviewees is important, too. A key building might have been designed by someone who is no longer alive, in which case interviews with their partners or even students might reveal something of their character.

Specialist users such as reception staff, security guards and maintenance crews all have a unique contribution to the account of the life of a building. Expert or professional responses are potentially much more detailed, but the purpose of non-professional expertise is different: it gives you access to the quotidian functioning of the spaces designed by architects. It is important, therefore, to recognize users' expertise in their own everyday lives and professions, even if their level of knowledge about architecture might be somewhat less detailed. This sort of data has to be carefully elicited so that respondents include the details of their everyday lives that they themselves might consider to be relatively insignificant.

You must also consider how many people to interview. By and large, this decision needs to be determined by the kind of research being conducted. Investigations of user groups and other non-expert groups might rely on larger samples, for example, in order to gather results that can be aggregated in some way: larger trends only emerge reliably from sample sizes containing tens or hundreds of responses.

Networking and permission

Gaining access to interviewees can be a significant barrier, particularly as it is both somewhat inconvenient and disruptive to everyday life. Some interviews with individuals and smaller groups of people can be arranged through personal contacts and networks, of course, but this relies upon your ability to make contacts effectively: something that is rather fraught as a student or early-career researcher. Membership of both formal and informal associations at local and national level can help enormously. These can include associations of architects in a particular city or region, as well as groups that associate around a particular topic such as sustainable design, architectural history or urban design.[1]

Official letters explaining your position as a researcher associated with a particular university department or architectural office can give people confidence in your intentions. It is important when writing to the gatekeepers at organizations who can give access to larger numbers of interviewees that you validate your research and are clear about its intentions and process. People need to know that you are not wasting their time, and your affiliation will reassure them. Second, you must outline what your research is about, and explain why you would like to interview individuals from their particular organization. The covering letter should provide the contact details of a lecturer or line manager who is responsible for your work, as well as some details about the kind of interview, the degree of anonymization, and an estimate of how long each interview should take. Giving details such as these is only fair to your potential interviewees, allowing them to make an informed decision about whether or not to participate.

Remember at all times that you are asking people to volunteer their time and expertise, so you should act accordingly, and treat this information as valuable – and remaining the property of the interviewee.

Testing

Preparation is important when conducting any kind of interview, and it is advisable to have a test run of your methodology and questions.

This is part of a careful planning process that allows you to get the most out of your interviewees. The better prepared you are going in, the more relevant information you will get from the interview. One way of preparing is to ask friends and colleagues for assistance, testing the questionnaire with them in order to find out which questions are most effective, where some might overlap with others, and to receive honest feedback from trusted peers. Honesty is crucial here: it is no help to have someone just reassure you that everything is perfect. You need critical input at this stage. Testing in this way helps to refine your approach by highlighting any redundant questions, and identifying where additional questions might be required for elaboration.

Types of interview

Interviews can take a number of different forms, as can the types of questions you ask within them.

Unstructured interviews and free-flowing conversations
The model of a free-flowing conversation is the basis of many face-to-face interviews, and also works with telephone and VoIP (e.g. Skype) conversations. Such freedom allows the interviewee to elaborate on topics that interest them, and to take the conversation off on a number of tangents. Such conversations have to start somewhere, however, so the interviewer must provide an initial question that will spark a long discussion. The interviewer must also be well read and well informed about their topic: this sort of discussion might take any number of paths, and the interviewer must be able to respond and react accordingly. It is good practice to have a number of questions in mind or written down for your informant to respond to. These can be tackled in any order, but they can be used to redirect a conversation that has gone off topic for too long. You should always remain mindful of how long your interviewee has scheduled to speak with you, too. However much the most enthusiastic interviewees will wish to speak on tangents, you must ensure that the interview addresses the topics relevant to your needs as much as possible, without curtailing the free flow of the conversation. This is aided by being up front about your topic from the outset.

Structured questionnaire-based interviews
Structured interviews are ideal for larger cohorts, where you are looking to identify trends from a variety of cross-comparable accounts. This collation of larger amounts of data can reveal much less specific, more general conditions, and this is an important, useful quality. The preparation for such larger-scale interviewing processes is substantially different from that needed for a handful of free-flowing conversations. First, the questions must be the same for every interviewee, potentially giving the actual interview a more artificial air. This can be constructed as a questionnaire that allows the researcher to conduct the interview by

purely written means. This can be helpful in automating your responses, allowing for much larger cohorts of interviewees, but it will also lessen the control you have over the process. There are fewer options for assessing the individual interviews in large studies, but that is generally not the point. Should more fine-grain or narrative data be required, then it is important to ensure that you supplement your structured interviews with a small number of more free-flowing ones.

There is a rising tendency to source interviewees online, using a range of tools and methods to gather responses. Services such as SurveyMonkey, FormSite or QuestionPro, or popular academic platforms such as Moodle and Blackboard, can be free to use (often with a limited number of questions), while signing up to other systems will only cost a small amount, which can be factored in to even the most modest research budget. The key here is finding a suitable cohort.

Advertising your survey via social media such as Facebook or Twitter can be a good start, as can going through your own contact list and asking for help in distributing the survey further. You need high-quality data, though, so it is important that this activity is carefully targeted. There is no point (and it is questionable ethically) in having family members contribute to a detailed survey about architecture unless they have experience in that area.

Focus groups

Focus groups are a variation on the interview that allows a group of participants to be addressed simultaneously. This is an excellent way to ask a series of questions related to a screening, physical object or series of images, where the exhibition of material and items is crucial to the data being gathered.

The main problem with focus groups is also their main benefit – that members might subscribe to a kind of group thinking and become influenced by one another. Such consensus is not automatically a bad thing, but it can skew your results if there is a particularly persuasive member of the group. A very carefully structured agenda can help to alleviate this. By programming the research in an orderly fashion, the interviewer remains in control of the situation and is better placed to ensure that useful data is provided.

Introduction: Outline the research project and its aims. Tell people what to expect from the session, how long it will last, the degree of anonymization, and explain how the data is to be used and published. Ask the participants to sign release forms at this stage.

Demonstration: Show the subject under discussion. This might be a product, a set of drawings, a short film or audio clips. Participants can provide their feedback here by way of written answers, using a questionnaire to elicit responses. Try not to allow discussion at this stage.

Discussion: A separate discussion session allows the focus group to provide the best of both worlds in terms of your data gathering. This can be recorded and transcribed much like a one-on-one interview.

Exit interviews and activity-based work

Some circumstances require an exit interview – for example, if you have facilitated a drawing or model-making workshop for people without architectural training. You might want to find out what they have learnt from the process, what expectations they had upon starting the workshop, and what surprised them once they had gone through the process. This can be achieved using any of the techniques above, but requires a different, structured set of questions in order to secure specific details about the activity.

As suggested by the name, exit interviews are conducted after the event, and should be conducted without the event facilitator being present. This is important as some respondents might feel less free to speak in the presence of someone with a strong stake in the workshop (even if they do not speak). Interviews can always be skewed if you are not careful. Something as simple as being present when you have clearly led a practical workshop might result in unintended consequences: you may get involved in a discussion about specific points, or your presence may discourage negative feedback.

Non-verbal interview techniques

Interviews thus far have been presented as verbal exchanges, but this need not be the case, particularly with architectural research. Innovative architectural interviews can involve drawings and model-making as primary modes of engagement. The most famous example of this is the mental mapping technique used by Kevin Lynch in his seminal work *The Image of the City*, where city residents were asked to produce maps of the cities they lived in.[2] You might use an existing drawing as a starting point, or ask your respondents to make a drawing using a particular convention or technique, such as a new piece of CAD software.

Non-verbal interviews are often backed up with verbal components, of course: only rarely will a single form of enquiry tell you everything you need to know.

Interviewing architects, who are often visual thinkers, will often involve drawings in order to demonstrate an idea. It is always a good idea to have some paper in order to discuss the finer points of an aspect of architecture. This poses some problems with regards to documentation, as you need to consider how to record not only the final drawing that is produced (often collaboratively) – but also the process by which it is drawn. Digital photography or video recording is a good way to do this. Photography is particularly ubiquitous, allowing you to respond to how an interview has progressed fairly organically, whereas video requires a little setting up, and can often distance your interviewee despite efforts to the contrary. Should the topic of your interview be specifically visual, such as in the drawing of maps, plans, etc., then it is worth considering setting up a tripod with video camera on the paper in order to record how, and in what sequence, marks are made.

Your questions

The phrasing of interview questions is crucial for establishing the kind of answers you will get. This process needs to be informed by your interviewees. Are you talking to professionals, community groups, students or someone else? Will some technical and theoretical language help you to communicate accurately and efficiently, or will it only serve to alienate your interviewee?

Questions can lead your interview and determine the results too strongly. This harms your research, and transfers your presumptions on to the process. Try to avoid polarized questions that give your interviewees too narrow a range of responses, particularly with regard to free-flowing conversational interviews. It applies a false dichotomy at times, and if you do use such polarized questions, try to make sure that these are on the basis of polarities that are known and expected within your demographic.

Preference questions are also problematic in this regard, as they often establish false choices between one kind of environment and another, or serve only to reinforce the presumptions of your interviewee.

For free-flowing interviews, when preparing your questions it is helpful to write one or two supplemental questions that will help draw more out of your interviewee. Some respondents are reluctant to talk, or self-edit things that they believe to be self-evident. You want to hear these answers, however mundane you – or the interviewee – might believe them to be. This reluctance is often overcome by rephrasing or supplementing your initial question with further, more detailed ones. Simply asking for elaboration is confrontational, and works against the idea of the interview unless you are very skilful as an interviewer, so prepare a stock of more finely grained questions that will help you to drill down, possibly ending with a request for an example in order to open up the conversation.

General, open: *What do you think about modernist architecture?*
These kinds of question can provide a good opening gambit, but you might find yourself with too wide-ranging a set of responses. Have you defined the terms by which you ask the question?

Leading: *Was modernism a necessary step in 20th century architecture?*
This is a leading or polarizing question, but can be useful to ask someone you know to be hostile to the question. You are asking if there are any redeeming features to this style and period of architecture.

Provocation: *Historians have argued that modernism opened up new options to architecture. Do you think that it was a positive influence?*
You can distance yourself from an opinion, but still ask for a response to it. This might be from a famous architect or historian, but the key is for the opinion to be identified as that of another person.

Devil's advocate: *Can you think of a positive example of modernism in the UK?*
Particularly useful when you know a respondent is antipathetic to the subject; you can turn the tables a little and ask for a positive example. Asking for examples can be a very good strategy for supplemental questions, but this kind of question directly challenges an interviewee, and may in fact harden their attitude. There's no way back if they answer 'no' to this question, unless you then proffer an example of your own.

Recording and transcription

Documentation is important with all research, and interviews are no different. Each type of interview has its own requirements, but you need to ensure that you keep records of each step of an interview process. If the interview is on paper or online, then you need to collect all of this information; if there are drawings or maps, these must be collated and scanned or photographed; if the interview was purely conversational, then you need to keep an audio or video record of this.

Each of these presents you with an organizational challenge, and also needs to be processed in some way. Audio of interviews must be transcribed, and while there is some software to help with this, it is most often a laborious process of typing up what was said in an interview, turn by turn.

Expect to spend a lot of time transcribing interviews, sometimes as much as an hour per ten minutes of spoken word. Your duty is to produce an accurate written representation of the conversation, with minimal editing, but removing any obvious stumbles and mistakes that were quickly corrected. You can use the interviews as extracts, much in the same manner as a quotation from a book, by citing the interview subject and date. It is good practice to include the full transcript as an appendix to your paper, but this might not always be possible or permissible due to word limits or the preferences of your interviewee.

Ensure that the date is given in your file names and folders when you store material, so that you can find the data in future. Interviews can be valuable resources that might speak to further research projects in future if they are open and wide-ranging enough, so treat them not simply as resources for your current project, but with an eye to their future usefulness, to yourself and even other researchers.

File names

Gather files into folders. Have a clear hierarchy of folders with the course title or project name at the top, followed by sub-folders which separate out data and working documents. One of these sub-folders should gather up the interviews, containing the audio files in one folder, and transcriptions in another. If you edit your audio in order to clean up the quality, remember to maintain a copy of the originals.

>*Research_guide*
    >*Interviews*
        >*Transcripts*
        >*Audio_recordings*
            >*Original_files*
            >*Edited_files*

Your file names should have the name of the interviewee and the date. As the use of certain punctuation has a specific role in digital file retrieval, it is wise to use short dashes in dates and underscores instead of spaces.

An example might be:
Lucas_Ray_20150206.wav

The order of information might appear somewhat counterintuitive here, as it is presented in the order of YYYYMMDD (year, month, day), and surname is placed before given name. When used consistently, conventions such as these allow for more effective searching at a later date.

Analyzing your interview

Your final task is to analyze the content of your interview. This can be conducted with reference to a theoretical framework, automated through software, or by simply reading it through carefully. For large samples of interview data, the initial step is to take all of the interviews together as a set, and to assess what kind of trends can be identified from the information you have. Data from questionnaires can be entered into spreadsheet software in order to produce statistical data from larger sample sizes. Your data might be diverse in this case, or show distinctive trends. Similarly, proprietary software such as NVivo can be used for detailed qualitative analysis of your interview. This analysis assists you in producing frequency analysis, producing a variety of visual representations including word clouds, colour coding and tree visualizations depicting a key word in a variety of contexts.

Individual interviews, with more detail, require close reading – and critical reading, similar to your literature review – as a methodology. This is much more qualitative than the generation of statistics above, but can give much richer information that is less absolute. Trends cannot be established from such interviews, but often this is not important: where the interviewee is a key practitioner, for example, and you are simply asking about their working practices.

Every interview process needs to provide your research with some data, so return to your interview questions as well as your research questions. Extract key trends or quotations from your data that challenge as well as support your position on the issues you are investigating, and discuss what this data tells you for your research topic.

Chapter 7: Writing up

Conventionally understood as the primary element of conducting research, writing is undeniably important, whatever form this might take. And crucial to any form of writing up is the structure of your argument.

It is important, too, to see your writing from the point of view of the reader, as it is too easy to become so close to the work that you make assumptions, or present information in the order it was discovered rather than the order appropriate to explaining it. This chapter offers some practical ways to ensure that your structure is rational, your narrative is clear, and your findings are presented in an orderly manner.

Disseminating your research is necessary if you are to engage in debate, share your thoughts and ensure the robustness of your findings. Good research has an audience, and interacting with that audience can help to further develop work, or suggest applications and subsequent work. Audiences might include professionals, academics, clients or stakeholders, and this chapter will look at the needs and interests of each, alongside ways of disseminating research via verbal presentations, exhibitions and various publications.

Key forms of publication shall be discussed, too, including journals publication and conference presentation, with a step-by-step guide to assembling your work, adapting content to match audience expectations, and making sure your research does as much work for you as it can. The chapter is then rounded off with a summary of some of the different citation conventions for footnotes and reference lists.

Knowing your audience

Your writing will always have a presumed audience in mind and, in a phrase that will crop up a few times in this chapter, you have a duty to your reader to ensure that your work is accessible and easy to read. This does not mean that your work is simplistic, but rather that it is appropriate to your audience: different degrees of technical language and styles of writing are appropriate to different audiences and purposes for your work, so it is important that you are mindful of this.

This relates largely to the tone of your writing. In an academic tone, for example, it is best to avoid colloquial language and other such imprecisions, as they can have a detrimental effect on the authority of your words.

If your essay or paper is for a university assessment, the best source for assistance is the assignment itself. This will typically provide information on what is expected of your work and how it will be assessed. Generally speaking, an essay needs to give its information in a manner that emphasizes the academic rigour of your investigation. To this end, keep the information in your essay relevant and close to the topic of your research question. It is very easy to wander off topic, to go off on tangents, and to provide extraneous information.

Any notable information that breaks the flow of what you are writing should be included as a footnote or endnote (see page 99). This mechanism in academic writing allows you to give further references – a definition of a term, an indication of some wider implications, or a deeper justification to a point you have made, all without interrupting another point or idea. Think of footnotes as short asides that demonstrate the extent to which you have a command of the general topic but without harming the focus of your individual essay.

All of this can appear a little dry for other audiences, who are not as interested in your need to justify opinions or validate the worth of your research. That is not to say that the rigour is not expected, just that the audience for a blog entry, magazine article or professional journal will have different expectations to the audience for an academic journal, book or university assignment.

These less formal means of communication can have a much friendlier tone, and give more opinion than academic writing. Not that this is licence to make sweeping assertions, unfounded opinions or unsupportable facts. Just that your audience in these circumstances does not need to know as much about the intellectual context of your argument as an academic. It is worth consulting the list of sources provided in Chapter 3 again (see page 53), but with an eye to your own writing:

Undergraduate assignments: Some undergraduate assignments will be designed to test your knowledge, ensuring that you have learnt the lessons from a seminar or lecture series. This is less common nowadays, as pedagogical thinking moves towards building skills for research rather than testing recall, so your assignment may well bear a more indirect relationship to the material covered in lectures, and ask you to conduct some original research of your own. It is crucial that the tone of an assignment is correct. Avoiding flippant use of language is crucial, as this has the potential to undermine your authority as an author. Sometimes it is important to address how you are saying something as much as what you are saying.

Postgraduate dissertations: There is a more stringent requirement for original research in a postgraduate assignment such as a Masters-level dissertation. Where you can work largely with existing knowledge at undergraduate level, it is important to begin making some novel or unique contribution at this higher level, where your work can be important enough to be placed in your university library's permanent collection, and made available for others to reference and cite.

PhD theses: The PhD thesis leads to the highest level of university degree, and has a formal requirement to be a unique and novel contribution to knowledge. The tone of a PhD thesis is strictly academic, and there is no place for playfulness, idiosyncrasy or assertion. This has to be a rigorous piece of work, as it is assessed in great detail by two examiners.

Reports: A report has more space for raw data, where much of the analysis is completed, but ultimate interpretations of that information are intended for someone else. Reports are heavy on content and light on argument, having the purpose of enabling someone else to come to decisions based on the clearest presentation of the available data possible. The introduction in this case can be replaced by an executive summary, which operates a little like a conclusion, but is situated at the head of the report as a shorthand guide to the information within. Reports typically enable others to make decisions and can be intended as persuasive documents, but are more often intended as neutral.

Peer-reviewed journals: Writing for a peer-reviewed journal requires a degree of discipline, as the style is prescribed by each publication. Check their requirements for submission and ensure that you are conforming to these. These requirements are sometimes very specific, and must be adhered to. This is one of the most demanding forms of academic writing, and must have strong arguments based on original research and a substantial literature. All of this must be evidenced within the paper to the extent that any other academic should be able to find each and every source you have used. Your audience might be specialists in a sub-field of your broader discipline here, so there is greater licence to use specialist language, or to presume background knowledge.

Edited collections: There is a lighter touch in terms of style when it comes to an edited collection, when compared to the peer-reviewed journal, but your editors will be the ultimate arbiters here. Publishers will have to approve and send the book out to review, so the arguments need to be strong, as well as fitting in with the overall concept for the collection. It is not good to strike out on your own in such a collection: your work must interact well with the other chapters and the overarching narrative of the book.

Academic monographs: Similar once again to the peer-reviewed journal, you have more control over the formatting of your academic monograph, particularly if you have a good working relationship with your editor. The editor is the contact point with the publisher, and will be able to advise you on writing style above and beyond the style guide provided by the publisher. Academic monographs are also peer reviewed and scrutinized at every stage, so it is important to ensure that your writing maintains an authoritative tone while being accessible to non-specialists within your field.

Architectural monographs: The architectural monograph is a curious form of publication that needs to focus on the context of the architects in question as well as giving accurate descriptions of their work. Once this job has been done, you can begin to consider the meaning and implications of their oeuvre, but this is not the place for a fully theoretical or critically informed reading of their work so much as an intelligent and passionate celebration of it.

Catalogues: Catalogues for exhibitions have an even wider audience, and should be designed with the non-specialist in mind. The interest of the reader can be counted on, but you need to give more time over to explaining any key ideas that come up, and direct your attention towards the meaning of the work, the intention of it, and explaining what you are communicating as clearly as possible.

Professional architectural press: In speaking to professionals, you will find that architects are interested in history theory, but often from the point of view of how it helps them to design and think about their own work. There might be greater emphasis on the materiality and process of constructing a building when giving an account of it, but there is also greater space for critique. The best articles in the professional press give avenues to explore and are full of possibilities without closing down with absolute and self-serving controversial conclusions.

Academic and experimental architectural press: Fuller freedom comes with publications at this end of the spectrum to the extent that the lack of implicit rules can become problematic in itself. Consult earlier editions of the publication and discuss your ideas with the editors, but this is often a good place to test ideas out, and to exploit the freedom of the discipline of architecture most fully.

Architectural firms' websites: You might be called upon to contribute to an architectural practice's website. The tone here is determined by the partners in the firm, and needs to express the position statement, agenda or manifesto of the practice. This can be difficult to judge in isolation, so requires some clear parameters and regular checking with colleagues to ensure that you are not misrepresenting the firm.

Blogs and website contributions: Personal blogs and contributions to more established websites can be a place to exercise some freedom in your presentation of written and visual materials. This might take the form of a position or polemical piece, expressing your opinion and your opinion only; interviews can be presented in full with only the barest introductory material, and all manner of experimental forms of discourse can be presented. The main limitation is the attention span dedicated to such web sources, which tends to be much shorter than published texts: brevity is important when expressing your opinions online.

Your duty to the reader: structuring your writing

Most forms of academic writing will conform to a structure that consists of *introduction*, *development* and *conclusion*. Each chapter and each section of each chapter should follow a similar pattern. This might feel repetitive, but it assists the reader in understanding your argument. Your duty is to the reader of your work, enabling them to follow your argument without too much trouble.

The introduction must set out the terms of enquiry for the chapter that follows, the terms used, the questions asked and the context approached. Following this, your development represents the main body of the chapter, whatever the topic. Your conclusion can summarize the main points or actually begin to draw some interim conclusions. These interim findings can build from one chapter to another, towards the essay's main conclusion.

Different chapters will also have different roles within your written work. Some of these are essential; others are optional, depending upon the topic you are tackling. Some essays and papers will require multiples of some chapter or section types.

Introduction
Despite appearing to be relatively self-explanatory, it is important to get your introduction chapter right. Even the shortest piece of writing requires an introduction, as you must assume that the reader is approaching your work fresh. You might presume a certain level of disciplinary knowledge – that you are writing for architects or people with a similar educational expertise, for example – but the topic itself will need some explanation.

Conventionally, your introduction should discuss your research question in detail, unpacking it and explaining some of the implications of your question. Your introduction also needs to discuss the context you are working in, be that a physical location, the work of a particular firm of architects or a historical period. The introduction should discuss some key terminology as part of this process. This lexicon can develop a unique position towards even the most everyday words.

If your word limit allows, then the final task of the introduction is to summarize the chapters that follow. This is particularly helpful in an introduction to a collected volume, where essays are contributed by a number of different authors.

Literature review

The literature review establishes an intellectual context for your writing. Some writers will thread elements of this through several chapters, making reference to texts as and when required. The benefit of a consolidated literature review near the beginning of your work is, however, that you can (as noted below with theory chapters) refer to these texts throughout your work if they are discussed early enough. The literature review can include methodological, historical, theoretical and other kinds of source that are relevant to your work. The distinction is that these should be texts that influence your reading of other contexts and phenomena.

Remember that you can have multiple chapters of a single type, so you might choose to have several distinctive literature reviews, perhaps one dealing with historical, one theoretical, one methodological; or even one chapter that gives a thorough account of the work of one theorist or architect. The literature review does not need to make too much effort to make this material relevant, as this can be handled in subsequent chapters.

Theory chapter

A distinctive variation on the literature review is a chapter devoted to theory. This often occurs in disciplines that devote a great deal of time and attention to fieldwork, where the narrative of the reportage is interrupted by the introduction of theoretical elements. It is important not to see this as a kind of compartment for the discussion of more fundamental or abstract ideas, however.

Your theory discussion should inform other chapters, and placing this chapter near the start of your work will allow you to refer back to it, most likely in the conclusion to other chapters.

Methodology

In addition to discussing potential methodological issues in your literature review(s), you need to address your own methodology. Again, this might be a short introduction to a further chapter where you discuss an activity in detail, but you need to make your methods clear, noting sources and giving a full account of precisely how you conducted your research.

Case or precedent study

Many chapters will fall into this category, as it can be used to discuss any topic. This is where your work explores the substance of the research question, so several interconnected chapters will commonly be used to explore the cases or contexts you are investigating.

Primary data: interviews and fieldwork

The style of a fieldwork chapter will differ significantly from the above, and will often have a narrative flow to it that sets it out as a distillation of field notes, or series of observations interspersed with direct quotes from interviews. The directness of the engagement is foregrounded in such chapters, and while theory need not be absent completely, it often takes a back seat in such chapters or sections. You want your context or your interviewees to speak for themselves in a chapter like this.

Conclusion

The conclusion is one of the most important parts of your work, as it is here that you have the opportunity to speak for yourself. Having assessed the evidence and data in your work thus far, you may, with authority, tell the reader what you believe to be the case, the implications or the meaning of your topic. Without a sufficient conclusion, your reader may be left asking what the point of your research is.

With this in mind, the conclusion is a chapter that speaks outside the confines of the essay and tries to discuss the wider implications and importance of what you have discussed. Why is it important, for example, to survey a particular historical period or understand different concepts of dwelling, or the uses of architecture in contemporary fiction? One way to begin this is to summarize your interim conclusions. Each of your development chapters can draw conclusions as it goes along, building towards the end of the essay, where you get to draw all of these observations together into a more unified whole.

Appendix

Appendices are useful, but should be used sparingly, as you cannot guarantee that your reader will refer to the information contained within. Supplemental information can be presented in your appendices, such as complete transcripts of interviews, fuller accounts of projects and experiments, further data sets or illustrations. You should not attempt to use appendices to add further chapters to your essay; they are not a licence to circumvent the word count, but rather a way of supplementing the essay with some of the raw evidence and data you have gathered in a more coherent and self-contained form. This then allows you to refer to the documentation within the essay.

Glossary

Too much jargon and specialist terminology should generally be avoided, but it is often essential to your argument. Examples might include an account of a national architecture with specific terminology that your audience will not necessarily understand. Other examples include times when you use terminology in very specific ways, and need to keep the definitions together in one place. This should not replace your account of this terminology within the context of the essay, but rather should perform the function of gathering these definitions together.

Referencing and citations

Referencing is a source of consternation among many undergraduate students, who worry about the formatting or citation styles and the fraught relationship with plagiarism. The aim of referencing is not to make the task of the writer more difficult, but to present essential information in a common format that allows your reader to understand where your information and ideas have come from. Simply put, referencing is giving credit where credit is due.

One of the most misunderstood facts about citation is that using references and placing your work within the context of an existing academic literature actually strengthens your work. The persistent myth of the individual genius does us all a great deal of harm in this regard, but it is worth underlining that referencing the texts relevant to your study can only improve it.

Referencing is a diligent activity, and allows you to present your reading of the existing scholarship in a particular field of study or discipline. Every reader brings something new to each text – even to your writing – and it is important for you to present the sources of your work, and to understand that you bring a unique perspective and understanding to these resources. This allows other writers to take issue, to find new insights and to understand precisely what you mean when you discuss a concept, theory or idea.

There are a wide range of different citation styles, but they have certain things in common. Each style gives the information below:

Author name: The key information is who wrote something. This allows us to understand a text's place in a broader body of work, and to source their thoughts on other issues. It is not enough to give the name of the book itself, as there may be several books of that name, and this would also indicate that you see this text as something absolute and immutable rather than the work of an author, or group of authors. If a shorthand is to be used, then the author's surname is the accepted norm.

Editors: This information is used in the place of the names of authors when an entire edited collection is cited. It is better practice to give the individual contributions and to attribute these to the authors concerned; citing more than one article from a single collection is fine.

Publication title: An obvious indicator for what you have read, it is often more helpful to give the journal article or chapter title of a specific contribution to a journal or collection of essays rather than the title of the collection. In this case, the common notation is to give the title in quotation marks rather than using italics.

Publisher & place of publication: Practical information on who published the text is an aid for finding the text.

Publication date: This information can be presented in a number of ways, but the year of publication might be much later than the original date of writing. Give the date of the version of the book you used. If you feel it is important, then give the original date of the text in square brackets, but it is helpful for a reader who is interested in your sources to know that edition or pressing of the text you are using, particularly as your citation may include page numbers.

Page numbers: Where you are quoting directly, this is essential; where you are referencing a broader argument it is preferable.

Date accessed: For online sources, websites can change with no notice, so it is important to state the date when you last accessed this information.

Web sources: A URL is not enough here, as you need to be able to give similar information as for a print publication; even if the author is unknown or anonymous, you need to state this explicitly. More often than not, when this information is missing, you can still give a corporate identity to the information – for example, citing the RIBA as the author of the information if no individual author is named.

There are a variety of ways to reference and cite another writer's work. The most direct is to use quotations. These must be indented or enclosed in quotation marks in order to mark them out as written by someone else. For short quotes, these can appear in-text, in the flow of the essay you are writing. Quotations longer than a line of text should be separated out as a paragraph and indented. In both cases, the author and text needs to be credited with a citation directing the reader to the reference list. This would take the form of (Lucas 2013:45) to mean the text in the bibliography written by R. Lucas in 2013, page 45. Different forms of citation handle this slightly differently (see box), but the principle is the same.

This same short citation can be used when you refer to a broad argument of another author, or wish to cite them as the source of information without actually quoting them.

Compiling your references as you go along is best practice, and prevents you from having to reformat each of your citations and references in one sitting at the end of your project. Consistency in your referencing format is important, and can be assisted through the use of software such as EndNote, which most universities will have licences for.

Anxieties over plagiarism should not dominate your thoughts, as it is very easy to avoid. The aim of referencing is to ensure that you are making best use of the wide range of academic literature at your disposal, placing your investigations in a wider academic context, and recognizing the ideas and thoughts that will help you to develop your own position. This is not to deny you your opinion, as you are still free to disagree and argue with such established positions, but it is important to know precisely what these positions are in order to articulate your own point of view with authority.

Citation examples

Your assignment or publisher may specify a particular referencing format. Every style of citation and referencing is equally valid, but it is important to conform to the style requested to give a degree of consistency. A wide variety of these are used, so the examples are restricted here to two of the most commonplace.

Harvard style (author–date system)
Bibliographic reference:

Koolhaas, R. (1994). *Delirious New York*. New York: Monacelli Press.

In-text citations are handled as a cross-reference to the bibliography/ reference list in this style:

Where the flow of your text includes a direct quotation such as 'this quotation is placed in single quotation marks followed by the author's surname and the date of the publication' (in Koolhaas 1994:200).

Chicago style (notes and bibliography)
The *Chicago Manual of Style* recommends using either the author–date system, or notes and bibliography, as below.

Bibliographic reference:
Koolhaas, R. *Delirious New York*. New York: Monacelli Press, 1994.

In-text citations are handled as footnotes in this style:

Where the flow of your text includes a direct quotation such as 'this quotation is placed in quotation marks followed by a superscript footnote number[2]', the number refers to a footnote reference that is formatted with a page number at the end:

2 Koolhaas, R. *Delirious New York*. New York: Monacelli Press, 1994, p.200.

Citing varied sources
All forms of citation practice allow a variety of texts and sources to be cited, each with different rules.

Single-authored book:
Koolhaas, R. *Delirious New York*. New York: Monacelli Press, 1994.

Multiple-authored book:
Lakoff, G. *&* M. Johnson. *Metaphors We Live By*. Chicago: University of Chicago Press, 1981.

Edited book:
Leach, N. (ed.). *Rethinking Architecture: A Reader in Cultural Theory*. London: Routledge, 1997.

Individual chapter in a book:
Lucas, R. 'The Sketchbook as Collection: A Phenomenology of Sketching', in Gittens, D. (ed.). *Recto-Verso: Redefining the Sketchbook*. Farnham: Ashgate, 2014, pp.191–206.

Journal paper:
Lucas, R. *&* O. Romice. 'Assessing the Multi-Sensory Qualities of Urban Space' in *Psyecology*, Volume 1, Issue 2, 2010, pp.263–76.

Government paper:
GREAT BRITAIN. *Homes for Today and Tomorrow: Elizabeth II*. London: Her Majesty's Stationery Office (HMSO), 1961.

Archive material:
James Stirling (firm), 1963–67, *History Faculty Building, University of Cambridge, Cambridge, England*. [Axonometric drawing] James Stirling/ Michael Wilford fonds. AP140.S2.SS1.D26.P3.1. Collection Centre Canadien d'Architecture/ Canadian Centre for Architecture, Montréal.

Website:
Centre Canadien d'Architecture/ Canadian Centre for Architecture. 'Found in Translation: Palladio – Jefferson. A narrative by Filippo Romano', http://www.cca.qc.ca/en/exhibitions/2488-found-in-translation-palladio-jefferson (accessed 6 February 2015).

Newspaper article:
Wainwright, O. (2015). 'Philharmonie de Paris: Jean Nouvel's 390m spaceship crash-lands in France', *The Guardian*, 15 January 2015. http://www.theguardian.com/artanddesign/2015/jan/15/philharmonie-de-paris-jean-nouvels-390m-spaceship-crash-lands-in-france (accessed 6 February 2015).

Film:
Stalker, DVD, directed by Andrey Tarkovsky. UK: Artificial Eye, [1979] 2002.

Conclusion

Writing up is the public face of your research, and is often how it will be judged: how well you communicate your process and findings to an external audience. In many ways, however, the writing-up phase is the least creative aspect of the process, as poor data gathering and weak knowledge of the context or the literature cannot be rescued by beautifully written prose.

That is not to devalue the process of writing up, but rather to understand its place within research: as the consolidation and communication of what your research is about. Your text needs to carry the weight of authority, to convince with its rigour and to be both interesting and relevant to the discipline of architecture.

Good writing is persuasive, backing its ideas up with evidence and argument. It may provoke your reader to think differently, to investigate some of your sources more thoroughly, or to consider looking at their own context and processes differently. In writing your conclusions, once you have summarized your thoughts, give some consideration to the effect and impact you wish your research to have. Your detailed and meticulous research to date will then give you licence to make suggestions and to posit what the possible implications and uses of your work are. What does your research allow us to do or to think that might not have been possible before? What does your perspective offer designers and academics in the future? What new projects does it leave for you to pursue now?

The conclusion is a future-oriented element of your work, and discusses the aim of your research in a fashion that is relatively free of the necessity to justify, as that work has been completed elsewhere in your essay, through careful discussion of literature, theory and case studies, as appropriate. Having established this solid groundwork and gained the confidence of the reader, you have now earned the right to express your opinion and define your own position.

Chapter 8:
Material culture

Material culture studies is a branch of anthropology
and archaeology concerned with the biographies of
things – the objects, clothing and materials we come
into contact with every day. As one of the most
established and directly relevant forms of social
enquiry, it's a useful way to engage with architecture.

This chapter includes a review of examples from Arjun Appadurai, Ian
Hodder, Victor Buchli and Joseph Rykwert, important figures in the field
today, each of whom makes a contribution to our understanding of the
role everyday 'stuff' plays in our lives – and, crucially, how understanding
materials in this manner offers ways in to the social nature of things.
The chapter is rounded off with an example of my own work in this
field, examining the material culture of the urban marketplace in Seoul
and other South Korean cities.

The commodity status of things

Writing in the essay 'Commodities and the Politics of Value',
anthropologist Arjun Appadurai describes wider exchanges and their
relationship to the gift-giving theory of Marcel Mauss.[1] Appadurai's
concern is entirely with the material culture of exchange, following
movements, flows and exchanges of goods and items in order to find
biographies for them, affording the object the equivalent of a person's
life story.

This is not so controversial now as it was at the inception of material
culture as a distinctive subset of anthropology, but there are some
problems with the approach, particularly when you come into contact
with practice-based theory, which argues that the skilled process of
making and using objects cannot be ignored.

Page 102: The New Museum of
Contemporary Art in New York,
Studio SANAA, 2007.

Appadurai stresses that not only are there values assigned to objects in economic transactions, but also that there is an inherent value in such exchange practices themselves. It is crucial here to understand that the seemingly unrelated ethnographic data of faraway lands and their customs affords theorists such as Appadurai and Mauss the opportunity to consider gifts and other forms of exchange in the round as fundamental human practices. This means they need to understand the broadest possible forms of such exchange, and to use this understanding to form theories that encompass the whole of human experience rather than a wholly Westernized understanding of the concept. By working with such examples as the potlatch gift-giving festival of some Pacific Northwest indigenous cultures, an understanding of exchange is possible that takes account of many if not all similar activities, in which items are exchanged in accordance with value systems, reciprocal arrangements, hierarchies of status and competition.

Understanding such practices gives architects access to a knowledge of the world that accounts for the variety of activities that take place there as well as a much more fundamental understanding of the conceptual drivers of that practice, such as reciprocity and obligation; factors that might remain hidden to a non-critical eye.

> Let us approach commodities as things in a certain situation, a situation that can characterize many different kinds of thing, at different points in their social lives. This means looking at the commodity potential of all things rather than searching fruitlessly for the magic distinction between commodities and other sorts of things. It also means breaking significantly with the production-dominated Marxian view of the commodity and focusing on its total trajectory from production through exchange/distribution, to consumption.[2]

So we see that this biographical approach to objects is fruitful in exposing the circulation of things. Rather than seeing objects, things and materials as fixed, this theory understands them as being in motion from one state to another. The patterns of distribution are important to understand. What are the means and ways in which these things move from one person to another?

Appadurai gives the following schema to understand the implications of this:

> The commodity phase of the social life of any thing
> The commodity candidacy of any thing
> The commodity context in which any thing may be placed.[3]

This categorization offers three ways in which the commodity nature of a thing can be understood. These are complementary categories rather than a thing being one or the other, moving from one to three. We must rather understand all three aspects of the object at one and the same time in order to grasp its commodity nature. Here, we can understand the temporality (1), the conceptual (2) and the location or place (3) of a given commodity. The temporality of a commodity refers to the idea that one thing may at one time be considered a commodity, but later not. The purchase of an item that becomes part of someone's selfhood and which they then would not part with is an example of this. My spectacles are a commodity when I go to the optician to be fitted for them, but I would not sell them when I am short of cash. This is because they cease to be a candidate for commodity status due to their utility and specificity to my needs. This might change at some point if there were a secondary market for such items (which there is not).

The concept of the commodity context as described by Appadurai is perhaps the most interesting here, given that it speaks specifically to spatiality: to the architectural context among other factors.

> Finally, the commodity context refers to the variety of social arenas, within or between cultural units, that help link the commodity candidacy of a thing to the commodity phase of its career.... Dealings with strangers might provide contexts for the commoditization of things that are otherwise protected from commoditization. Auctions accentuate the commodity dimension of objects (such as paintings) in a manner that might well be regarded as deeply inappropriate in other contexts. Bazaar settings are likely to encourage commodity flows as domestic settings may not.[4]

We can easily understand that the context of a painting by, say, Picasso, would be different in an auction house, a car boot sale, a national gallery, a private home or a commercial gallery. The rules of exchange are entirely different, or even denied and resisted, in these spaces.

> Thus, commoditization lies at the complex intersection of temporal, cultural, and social factors. To the degree that some things in a society are frequently to be found in the commodity phase, to fit the requirements of commodity candidacy, and to appear in a commodity context, they are its quintessential commodities. To the degree that many or most things in a society sometimes meet these criteria, the society may be said to be highly commoditized.[5]

Appadurai continues to describe which contemporary capitalist societies can be defined in this manner, and the extent to which objects are available to be commodities. Appadurai continually refers to the *careers* of objects, and the extent to which they have the three hallmarks of being commodities at any given time.

In the Western city, exchanges happen in a variety of places, and a close analysis of these can yield interesting results. Take the way in which tickets are bought at transit sites such as subway systems and railway stations. Often, this is mediated by vending machines, as time is a factor and human interactions are reserved for more complex intercity journeys.[6] The ways in which waiting is organized in this context is also instructive, either with long queues or ticketing systems that call people to a desk some time after they take a number from a dispenser.

Marketplaces encourage haggling and negotiation in a way that chain stores tend not to allow. This is partly due to the authority of the shopkeepers in each circumstance. The typical shop worker does not have the power to alter prices, even in the case of a shop manager of a large national or multinational chain. A market-stall vendor, however, is often selling his or her own wares, which can allow some flexibility in pricing. Small craft fairs and markets selling handmade and carefully crafted goods are another case in point, where possibilities for commissioning works co-exist with the opportunity to buy goods directly from the people who make them.

Chain stores have convenience on their side, be they food stores or suppliers of electronics, clothes, books and other goods. These stores have an identity that is maintained from one branch to the next, allowing the customer to know roughly where things are, and to feel comfortable from one ubiquitous place to the next. Department stores are another case entirely, where the goods are high value, high status and treated like art objects to a degree. The elaborate window displays that are themed to go with the season are the introduction to this, but other elements, such as the way in which staff interact, or the rather more sparse population of clothing rails, all aids in building the atmosphere and aura of these stores as something special and expensive.

This is one critique you can begin to apply to a site that you are investigating within a design or essay project. What is the nature of exchange there and how is the appropriate atmosphere achieved? The sudden appearance of seasonal markets across Manchester in December each year, when foodstuffs and crafts are sold in small huts stretching across the city centre, offers a contrast with the established central shopping district. Similarly, pop-up stores selling vintage or up-and-coming designers' clothing generate a temporality and rarity – one must be 'in the know', connected to the relevant networks in order to be aware of when and where such stores are going to appear.

Appadurai considers his overall project at the end of the essay:

> Apart from learning some moderately unusual facts and regarding them from a mildly unconventional point of view, is there any general benefit in looking at the social life of commodities in the manner proposed in the essay? What does this perspective tell us about value and exchange in social life that we did not know already or that we could not have discovered in a less cumbersome way? Is there any point in taking the heuristic position that commodities

a
b

c
d

e
f

g

Examples of different forms of economic exchange in a city: a) informal street traders in Madrid; b) a delicatessen in Rome; c) the Mercado San Antón in Madrid; d) NoHo Market in New York, occupying a vacant lot between buildings; e) the Barras Market in Glasgow; f) the kimono department in a Tokyo depato (department store); g) the density of shopping options in Gangnam, Seoul.

exist everywhere and that the spirit of commodity exchange is not wholly divorced from the spirit of other forms of exchange?[7]

This expresses the importance of exchange at the heart of value, commodification, commercialism and globalization. The exchange is what is important and fundamental, that which can be broken down into elements and spheres of influence. The broad politics of this are drawn from the work of social theorist Georg Simmel, and applied as a proposition around which the essay is framed. In the same way, we can begin to apply this critique and others found within this lecture, to a site we are interested in from an architectural point of view. This critique provides a way to understand a site of commerce, of exchange.

We have seen that such politics can take many forms: the politics of diversion and of display; the politics of authenticity and of authentication; the politics of knowledge and ignorance; the politics of expertise and of sumptuary control; the politics of connoisseurship and of deliberately mobilized demand. The ups and downs of the relations between these various dimensions of politics account for the vagaries of demand. It is in this sense that politics is the link between regimes of value and specific flows of commodities.[8]

Entanglements of people and things

Property signs around the High Line in New York. The rapid gentrification witnessed around this linear park runs counter to the community spirit that brought the project to fruition, but such is the draw of the eventual attraction that property has become extremely valuable, pushing many who had been living in the area further out from the centre of the city.

The archaeologist Ian Hodder writes about the ways in which people are *entangled* with material objects. He notes that it is a common mistake to talk about *things* as if they are ever isolated from engagement with people or other things:

A house wall needs a roof if the human need for shelter is to be fulfilled, a bath needs a plug, a sail needs a mast. Material things fit into each other so that if I place a large squared and flattened stone on another

it will stay there, at least long enough to make a wall. Things stick to each other. They can be tied together. Soap needs water, cooked food needs fire, iron ore needs a furnace if I wish to make metal.[9]

This is another occasion where considering the biography of materials is helpful: not as an inert and unchanging phenomenon, but as a point in a continuum, each point of which has something to tell our research.

Procurement: This refers not only to the purchase of the raw material, but to how it is obtained in the first place: for example, is it mined, farmed or otherwise sourced?

Manufacture: The processes by which something is rendered useful, by transforming a raw material into one with more affordances, crafting these materials into appropriate shapes, and forming assemblages of components into discrete units.

Use: The manner in which something is utilized, which can have a great deal of variation in the case of timber, fewer affordances in the case of brick, and very specific uses in terms of prefabricated units.

Maintenance and repair: All materials degrade over time. Sometimes this is because elements are worn down by rain and sunshine; in other cases pollution or repeated use cause wear and tear. How a material is to be maintained and kept in use is an often overlooked issue, but a pertinent one for architectural research.

Discard: Is an element or material beyond reuse? If so, how and where do we discard it? What is the immediate environmental impact of this discard, and what stocks remain of this material? How do we dispose of buildings, and what are the sociocultural implications of this?

Other processes are mentioned throughout by Hodder, and this is the key to his understanding of material culture: as part of a process, continually in flow and in relationships rather than in isolation. Things depend on each other, depend on people, depend upon relationships and entanglements. Elucidating these entanglements is one way of conducting relevant and valuable architectural research.[10]

Stuff as cultural indicator

Material culture theorists examine the relationships people have with objects, the places such objects may hold within their social encounters, and the meanings we attach to things.

Problems emerge with this when we begin to think about objects in other terms, and to consider the production of things – of the creativity

The New Museum in New York by Studio SANAA is an example of modest materials being used with a care and attention that elevates them to the finest timber and stone constructions. This is one way in which architecture can discuss and play with notions of material culture knowingly as a part of the design process.

fundamental to human life – as an important area of study. Material culture studies do begin to understand the life cycle of an object more fully, such as in Suzanne Küchler's account of the *Malanggan*, a ritual object from Melanesia that is later abandoned and collected by Western art dealers.[11] Objects are made and disposed of, but the processes of making are often discarded in material culture studies, problematically in the case of Alfred Gell's study of *Art and Agency*, which reduces the production of a painting, for example, to a set of social relations and economic transactions, completely sidestepping the notion of what the intention behind the actual production of the image is, and the process by which a set of experiences might find their way on to canvas.[12]

It is clear, however, that this approach to objects as fundamentally social is important. More than merely superficial, accounts of material, such as the study of clothing, speak directly to the experience of people's lives. Daniel Miller explores this in an accessible manner by looking at the literature on the topic of the sari worn by many Indian women.[13] The sari holds a number of cultural signifiers, relating to concepts of femininity ranging from motherhood to courtship, and including many anxieties about controlling the garment, keeping it in place, and of projecting a number of different images of the wearer. Miller couples this cultural significance with descriptions of the practicalities of wearing one, with its complex arrangement of pleats.

A more direct architectural example is the work of anthropologist Victor Buchli in examining the post-Soviet Russian home, as well as the historical context of the idea of homes under Communism.[14] According to Buchli, the style of home and the very concept of home was closely tied to the politics of the time, varying from a modernist agenda before Stalin moved the state architecture towards a stripped-down classicism that extended into the home. This again swung to a more spare style post-Stalin, before embracing global consumerist culture on the break-up of the Soviet Union. Each shift is significant in terms of how one is supposed to live according to each era, and represents the interaction between citizen and state, particularly when adaptations are required, or suggestions circumvented in inventive ways.

What Buchli describes is a complete politics of the home with the minimum of means: that there was political intent behind such things as curtains, the placement of furniture and wall decoration sounds somewhat absurd at first. This is worth holding on to. It is absurd, but a machinery of apartment overseers enforced this changing aesthetic, limiting the control people had over their own accommodation.

Buchli uses the Russian term *byt*, which loosely translates as 'lifestyle', but also contains the material trappings of that lifestyle. The control of *byt* was understood by the Communist Party to be incredibly important in striving for the Communist State: an important change in people's expectations and engagements with their homes away from the petit-bourgeois attitudes of homeliness. This consideration of home life is both rich in detail and of real importance to architecture, despite the everyday nature of the material. It also demonstrates that a theory offers a frame within which to understand a particular problem, and that such *byt* theorists deployed their knowledge in a didactic and political way.

Case study: The cart as assemblage in Namdaemun Market, Seoul

This project is part of a wider investigation into the urban marketplaces found in South Korean cities such as Seoul, Daegu and Busan. These markets are vibrant and resilient parts of the urban fabric, intertwined with the more formal aspects of the city and, while appearing to be chaotic, are in fact highly ordered places. One aspect of this research has been to investigate the market carts as a unit of enquiry. These constitute a kind of informal architecture par excellence, one that creates architecture and urbanism largely without or despite the intervention of professionals. My question is: what can we learn from such occupations of space?

In situ drawing is often contrasted with *post situ* investigations. The immediacy of drawing while in a place is often celebrated above a retrospective drawing from memory, or a record such as a photograph, but there is an element of drawing that is a notation of experience, of spectatorship. Some things are missed *in situ*, and drawing *post situ* allows an extension of the temporal frame: a meditation.

In attempting to understand the market and its components, these drawings constitute examinations and interrogations of the scene.

Sections show variations of volumetric space, plans describe the various states of openness and closure within the space (drawn crucially in sequences rather than in isolation), while elevations explore the variations in how a common module is exploited by vendors. Eventual intentions are tied up with an axonometric sketchbook of carts: dissolving things only to build them up again. The *sketch* is followed by the *drawing*.

Paolo Belardi's *Why Architects Still Draw* describes a student project that involved conducting a survey of a shanty town and declaring it a 'sixth order' of architecture.[15] This has some echoes in the work of architectural historian Joseph Rykwert (see Chapter 10 for more detail on Rykwert's thinking, and his study of the 'original' house as well as the orders in architecture). The idea of conducting a detailed survey is often presented as mechanistic, but has rather deeper potential than this. Belardi seeks to reclaim this idea of survey as a fundamentally architectonic act, which mobilizes drawing as an explicit means of understanding a context.

> At one time or another, all of us have likely seen what architects work with every day, the three canonic architectural views of some building made of white stone: plan, section, and elevation. These representations, apparently the output of an enormous slice-and-draw machine, give us measurements in the x, y, and z axes. Belardi argues that it's important—especially in today's world—to add a fourth dimension, time, and even a fifth one, culture.[16]

The various investigations of the market cart demonstrate both its particles (the metal grids and castors, prefabricated carts) and the power infrastructure (common weighing scales and demarcated ground plane; temporary barriers and ad hoc tarpaulin coverings). Each of these things is modest enough in itself, but once entangled with one another and set within the sociocultural context of the marketplace, they gain meaning and form, contributing to what are arguably the most exciting and engaging expressions of civitas in South Korean cities.

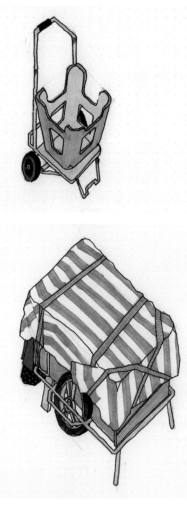

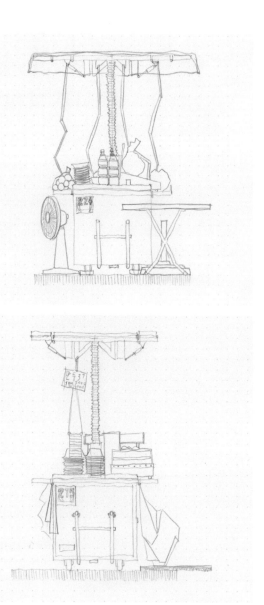

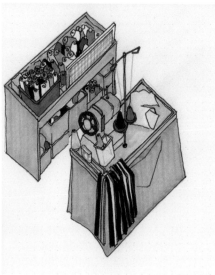

Drawings of carts from
Namdaemun Market in
central Seoul.

Chapter 9: Environmental psychology

An important field of research, environmental psychology has a great deal to offer architecture by investigating how people engage with the built environment.

Much of the field's methodology is strictly established by the field of psychology, requiring laboratory conditions and large numbers of respondents. Key sites for environmental psychology are educational and healthcare spaces, where the main users of those spaces have particular needs and are in a defined power relation. Psychology can give insights into people's preferences, evolutionary responses to space, and perceptions of safety or danger, and it can offer ways of improving wayfinding.

One of the largest fields of current research is into restorative environments, where psychologists contend that the richness of our built environment contributes to health in a number of ways. This chapter also presents some of the findings of 'Inflecting Space', a research project on the spatiality of the human voice, and how it operates as a determinant in public space.

James Gibson and alternative approaches to space

American psychologist James Gibson is a key figure in the understanding of sensory perception of space. Eschewing conventional psychology's preference for laboratory-based research, Gibson argued that perception of the environment could only be achieved while actually out in that environment. This ran counter to many practices, such as preference studies, where participants in experiments are shown images of environments in order to ascertain which ones they are more drawn to. Gibson's argument, followed by many afterwards, was that such practices can only tell us so much. Taken to their extreme, they can only really tell us what people think of photographs or screen-based images. This aside, there is a scientific rigour to the experimental method, which allows researchers to carefully construct experiments in the laboratory, so long as the intentions and claims made for that research are not too overstated.

According to Gibson, perception is not a static procedure where people are receptors, merely absorbing external stimuli. The model of *perceptual systems* that Gibson prefers takes the sense organ as a mobile, seeking organism, constantly searching for something to perceive.

Gibson further discusses the nature of the environment as divided into the *medium*, the *surface* and *substances*. This was a way of overturning the conventional notion of Cartesian coordinates, where space is abstract and arranged according to X, Y and Z directions. Gibson's model delivers an idea of our environment – that we are a part of, and cannot help but think within – as a medium that has thickness and quality. We breathe air, are choked by pollution, move through mud or swim in water. The substances are those elements that resist: conceptualized as solid by other models, but characterized as resistance by Gibson. Mediating between the two are surfaces, which can be permeable at times, permitting movement from one to the other.

This model of the world allows us to think more effectively about how we perceive the world and how it can affect us.

People-environment studies

People-environment studies are one field where psychology disciplines and the built environment come together. Several associations pursue this connection, such as the International Association for People-environment Studies (IAPS).[1] IAPS are committed to understanding the multitude of ways in which we engage with our environment, and what effect it has upon us.

This is a growing field of research, given the current discussions of restorative environments, where there is a position taken regarding the health of where we live. It has long been felt that our environment has an impact upon our health, but the nature of this relationship has been poorly understood. Organizations such as IAPS seek to understand this in a much more rigorous manner, and investigate a range of phenomena to better advise and design urban environments and architecture.

Moving beyond merely problematizing in the manner of 'sick building syndrome' and other pathologies, restorative environments research has a more positive outlook, seeking to understand optimum lighting levels, ideal uses of planting, visual clarity for wayfinding, and the kinds of places that people enjoy to take exercise in. Each of these contributes to the wellbeing of building users, in terms of both physical and psychological health.

Researchers use a variety of experimental methods, focus groups and interviews, longitudinal studies and other forms of data gathering and data mining in order to find out what the best ways of building are for a wide variety of different building users. This can often extend to user-centred design, where the people who are to use a building are given the opportunity to engage with the design process. This can lead to some issues around the nature of the designer and professional within the process, at worst being a process for validating the presumed design solution of an overbearing architect. At best, however, models of practice such as co-housing allow for collaboration between the people who will live in a place and the design team.

Such engagements are usually structured as workshops facilitated by the designers, who will have a narrow set of questions they will want to pose with each event. This might be to consider the context and how the building sits within it, identifying the needs of the community regarding access, security and sunlight. Another workshop might consider the materiality and finishes of the building: what the requirements of rooms are, such as bathrooms and kitchens, and which other outside consultants might be able to help.

The risk is that innovative solutions mightn't be possible from this type of consultation, but the fault will be in the design of the workshops that frame the collaboration, and not in the idea of consultation itself. As with all things, there are good practices and bad ones.[2]

Case study: 'Inflecting Space'

The 'Inflecting Space' project illustrated some of the methodologies and findings of this kind of enquiry. The idea that space is *determined* rather than pre-existing is one that warrants further discussion. One of the ways in which this can be achieved is through a questioning research project like this one, which was an investigation into the impact of the human voice in an urban context, as a spatial determinant.

The project was an Arts and Humanities Research Council (AHRC) funded project run by the University of Edinburgh, a collaboration between the Architecture and Music Departments. As a pilot study, the project had a great degree of latitude and fed into subsequent research in a number of ways. The project used multiple research methodologies

The project 'Inflecting Space' considered sites such as Waterloo Station in London, investigating the way in which voice determines public space.

over the course of a 15-month period in order to investigate the idea that we use our voices to determine or otherwise define spaces in the city.

The example that was returned to time and time again was the railway station, as this responded well to the theories we were approaching – pertinent to sound design in cinema, but useful in this context – of French film theorist Michel Chion.[3] Chion's work considers the currency and potency of the off-screen voice, the power that speech can gain when its source is impossible to discern. This is described in cinema theory as a kind of *voice of authority* circumstance, where a special agency is granted to this off-screen voice, whether they are considered a separate narrator or as a character within the story. This theoretical framework then informed the discussions across music (Peter Nelson), sound design (Martin Parker) and architecture (Richard Coyne[4] and myself).

One phase of the project involved data gathering, using digital audio recorders and binaural in-ear microphones, the effect of which was to reduce any in-device noise when recording, and also allow for recordings that replicated the stereo effect of a space to the extent that a listener with a trained ear could tell a great deal about that space by listening to the recordings. A series of environmental recordings were made and supplemented by other, more contrived recordings that allowed certain qualities of voice to be explored.

Two key exercises allowed us to discuss the qualities or *grain* (as described by Roland Barthes as 'the encounter between language and a voice') of the voice with participants.[5]

The first exercise was a series of focus groups and structured interviews, where participants were asked to respond to the recordings and media

Recordings from a variety of sources, including from this department store in Japan, were used as part of the process of explaining how much people could understand from an audio playback.

we had prepared. The conversations were recorded and transcribed, with key quotations used to illustrate points and to arrive at some of the research findings. Our focus group collaborators were given soundscapes to listen to and a series of questions to answer about the impression of space that they were given by the recordings. Different environments were contrasted with one another, and a series of individual interviews were followed by focus groups with different participants.

Focus groups can result in participants agreeing with one another, ironing out the differences in opinion and subsequently reaching a kind of mean.

Transit spaces, such as railway stations, can be understood as a collection of voices: the public address system, the authority of station staff, the informal and excited discussions of travellers with each other or on their mobile phones. Each demographic defines its territory through the use of their voices. Station announcements are ambient in nature and are equally present throughout the space, something that listeners to audio recordings noted as being particularly difficult to locate.

This interview with two fellow academics demonstrates some of these difficulties and how they can become framed as research questions:

> **DM:** To me that is partly what I felt uncomfortable about, sitting listening to that. You're almost deprived of that sense of – it is such a fluid space – and either me standing, as you were saying, say people come past you – making that connection between what this guy is saying and where he's going and me maybe rushing through and picking up a little bit of a conversation here and there – being deprived of that movement it is almost very difficult to piece together or make some sort of relation between these things.
>
> **RL:** It is interesting that you mention being deprived of the 'movement' itself rather than the visual element of it.
>
> **DM:** I have to say that I found it hard to do the visualizing, somehow represent ... there seemed to be some richness missing, and of course you've heard it all before, you know we've all been in those spaces – I was really struggling with that; I think that's what it was.
>
> **RL:** Does the fact that I was actually moving through the space make that more difficult, then? Or would a static recording have allowed you to understand the space?
>
> **DM:** I don't think so – you quite simply don't know.
>
> **DF:** In my head we were standing still, and in that case when a voice

gets louder and more full, you just think someone is walking up beside you and then he's going away. In this case it could have been that you were walking and he goes alongside you – then he veered off. There are different ways you can interpret your relationships – it's really interesting...

(Extract from transcript of listening session with DM & DF)

This recording was contrasted with a busy Tokyo department store, which was also recorded on the move rather than from a static position. A repeated call and response was being made by two of the staff members, who were working together, one male and one female. Despite their contrasting physical size and patterns of inflection, the two complemented each other, with the man making attention-grabbing calls of 'Good morning' and 'How may I help you?' in a deep, booming voice, while the woman called out in shrill tones, giving more information on the products in the sale that they were promoting.

DM: I didn't notice anything else that stood out all that much – they were definitely very overpowering. And because you hear them all the way through until the very end, there was something quite comforting about that – that familiarity – something that went all the way through. Listening to it, you could constantly hear them. You felt like you were moving, but you could always hear them – always in the distance, right up until almost the very end, and there was something nice about that, you could relate to that – sort of 'Okay that's those guys from the beginning'.

RL: So that gave you a sense of movement in the space, do you think?

DM: It did give me a sense of movement, but more than that – the first one: I did feel that sort of disorientation with these things sweeping in and out of you, but this one there was always that sort of reference sound. It felt very linear, but that's just I think because I could hear those people always – their voices were always there and would kind of pop up.

(Extract from transcript of listening session with DM & DF)

Despite the unfamiliar language and setting, this recording was found to be less difficult or jarring than the more familiar Waterloo Station. This might seem a little surprising. The key here is that the sound had a discernible source – not a *visible* source, as the participants in the session had not yet been shown photographs or videos – but a sense of space was created by the way that the voice carried in space, and eventually decayed. We could consider this the sonic equivalent of perspective. This decay of the voice that is expected by the ear was not present in the station; the announcement pervaded the whole space. A listener expects a sound source to be apparent, and is disturbed when it is not. This is one differentiation between ambient and located sounds. We are disturbed when something that ought to be a point source sound assumes the character of ambient sound – the ambient voice sounds like Chion's 'voice of authority'.

Visualizing this space was one of the tasks set as part of the listening session. This is, of course, a very difficult task, especially if undertaken without knowing what a railway station concourse looks like.

> **RL:** Actually visualizing the space – that was very difficult, then, for you?
>
> **DM:** Yeah, I found that very … I sort of resorted – it just seemed to me I was looking for different imagery that would somehow represent what I was trying to convey and there was nothing. It was difficult drawing anything that was going to do it justice, I just had this – it just seemed like this plain.
> I wouldn't say the space was coming across as something three dimensional with layers: it just seemed to be a plain in that one – something would sweep over you from one direction and then something would sweep back across from another and you just seemed to be in the middle of these things kind of sweeping – and you were moving in and out of them, they were kind of sweeping over you and then off into the distance again and something else would sweep in from another direction, and back out again – in a tidal-like way. Very … almost being swamped in these sounds.

(Extract from transcript of listening session with DM & DF)

Territory is defined in different ways in this context. Given the difficulties, however, some of these are unsuccessful in holding attention. One example of this was an information desk in the form of an island in the middle of the station concourse. Formally, this was little more than an office chair and small podium with the ubiquitous 'i' symbol hanging from the station roof – a situation that was shown to be unsuccessful and unsatisfying for station users in need of information. The characteristics of the space are described in some interviews as hollow tubes, and qualities of envelopment and immersion feature prominently in accounts of our recordings of reverberant, ambient, non-directional sounds. The ambient noise as well as public announcements or loud customer conversations drowned out this necessary service, crowded with confused tourists and other station users in need of assistance. This underlines the effect of poor or ill-considered sound design upon a space, demonstrating the way in which the methodology of recording and analysis can inform design. Further consideration of more effective positioning of sound sources could be tested and modified to create a more effective station.

The study identified inflection as a crucial quality for the study of urban soundscapes, which often focus on the content of speech or the pitch and amplitude of sounds. Inflection can be understood as the melodic movement of the voice from high to low frequencies, describing the variety and rate of change in the tones used. It became clear that voices with a varied pattern of inflection are more interesting to listen to, but inflection is also more complex than this. A regular pattern of inflection, for example, assists legibility, and we observed an important role for repetition across a variety of environments. It can also be observed that, when in a busy environment, voices grab attention and are deployed to maintain that interest. In these contexts, maintaining an even tone can be helpful in encouraging a listener to pay attention to a particular set of frequencies and continue a conversation. Two people quickly match the characteristics of their voices, and can effectively compete with much louder sounds by means of inflection.

All human beings learn to relate sound to distance in the act of speaking. We alter our tone of voice from soft to loud, from intimate to public, in accordance with the perceived physical and social distances between ourselves and others. The volume and phrasing of our voice as well as what we try to say are constant reminders of proximity and distance.[6]

The research project used MAX/MSP software to develop a custom application to analyze vocal inflection. The graphs produced are called melodramas, depicting changes in inflection rather than frequency or amplitude (loudness). This bears similarity to Barthes's notion of the *grain* of the voice:

> It is this displacement that I want to outline, not with regard to the whole of music but simply to a part of vocal music (*lied* or *mélodie*): the very precise space (genre) of *the encounter between a language and a voice*. I shall straightaway give a name to this signifier at the level of that, I believe, the temptation of ethos can be liquidated (and thus the adjective banished): the *grain*, the grain of the voice when the latter is in a dual posture, a dual production – of language and of music.[7]

A standard amplitude graph showing one of the audio samples from the 'sound studio' application by Felt Tip Inc.

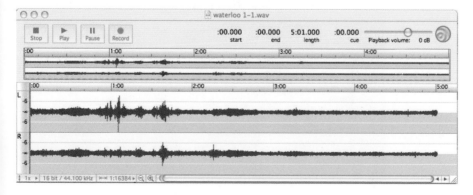

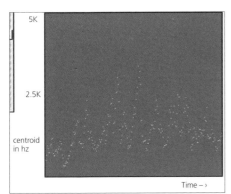

Above: Customized software describing the inflection of a sound sample – in this case, of a Shinjuku shop with rising inflection over time.

The visual and geometric aspects of any environment only ever tell us a portion of the story. Our voices are an important element in defining territory and constructing a sense of place; the human voice is one way of demonstrating agency over a place, a sense of control and presence in space.

These interview and focus group events helped us to design a series of sound installations to further explore the potential for sound design in architecture. The most substantial of these, titled *Vocal Ikebana* after the Japanese art of flower arranging, reused our environmental recordings, mounted on movable speakers in a white gallery space with some props. Participants in the sound installation were asked to listen to and respond to the various banal sounds we had chosen, and then to arrange the room in a pleasant manner (despite the deliberately dull and repetitive nature of the recordings).

Photographs from the *Vocal Ikebana* sound installation.

The participants could move the speakers and alter the volume, and they had crates to give height to their arrangement or to visually and aurally mask a speaker. There were throw rugs to absorb sound or define spaces, and some chairs and low tables.

The results of the experiment were extremely interesting, as a number of trends began to emerge.

Static arrangements

Some participants designed their room to be appreciated from a single position, as a kind of auditorium experience, or focused listening experience. This was usually denoted by the positioning of a chair and the use of the acoustics of the room to help create interesting effects with the recordings.

Prescribed path arrangements

Setting out a defined path was another common result, often noted on a plan that our respondents were asked to draw with arrows or numbers. This prescription had a developed narrative to it, a directionality and an order. This exploits the temporality of sound as a phenomenon that cannot be apprehended as a whole or totality.

Field arrangements

The field arrangements were more free-roaming results. These were uncommon, but they did occur. These were less prescriptive, and gave a great degree of freedom to the visitor to the installation, suggesting points of overlap and isolation, but not instructing. The narrative was less present, but a distinctive non-visual spatiality emerged.

What became interesting was the role of the drawing in the process of sound design in the room. Asking our participants to reflect upon their arrangement, we asked them to draw the layout of the room once they had finished. What was unexpected here was the way that this prompted people to return to the room with a desire to change things. The drawing practice opened up the installation to further modification; the logic of the drawing offered opportunities and encouraged participants to adapt and alter their design.

This example is one demonstration of the role for environmental psychology and methods including field recording, interdisciplinary working, focus groups and installations as forms of enquiry. This allows for various means of diagnosing the urban condition – measured sonically in this case – to be mobilized into eventual design strategies and recommendations.

Chapter 10:
Architectural histories

The longest established form of architectural research is the study of architectural history, although the conventional Western bias of this is gradually being eroded by plurally intertwining histories of architecture rather than a singular history dominated by Eurocentric classicism.

This chapter presents and problematizes some of the available approaches to architectural history, recasting the history of architecture as an engaging, evolving and live process rather than a neutral presentation of 'facts'. Redefining architectural histories by looking at them through the lenses of class and social history, colonial and postcolonial conditions, or gender studies, for example, is important for a contemporary understanding of the field.

Histories other than those based on simplistic geography or nationality are also possible: the history of architectural representation, social histories of architecture, environmental history, and many more subdivisions in terms of typology or building material are worth pursuing for what they reveal about architecture today.

The question is, then, which history is appropriate to study, and how? Architectural histories all rely on sources, of course, so what are your primary sources for this work, what buildings and documents remain from the time of construction, and what are the key points in the life of your topic: how does it reflect the broader history of the place and how is the site implicated practically or symbolically in a given era?

The study of architectural history remains open to new approaches and interests, but it must maintain the rigour of good academic research, with a combination of sources – from accounts dating back to the time of a building's construction, to your own field visits, as well as histories written by others (*see also* Chapter 3 for advice on using

Page 124: Norman Foster's
30 St Mary Axe, popularly
known as the Gherkin, with
St. Andrew Undershaft Church
in the foreground.

archives). History is not neutral, and the bias of each contribution to knowledge must be acknowledged, even if not agreed with. This chapter discusses a number of alternative approaches from key figures in architectural history – Manfredo Tafuri, Colin Rowe, Robin Evans, Joseph Rykwert and Nikolaus Pevsner. Mapping a clear path through this allows architectural history to contribute something fresh to our understanding of the discipline. This chapter concludes with a study of the architectural manifesto and its trajectory from polemic stance to position statement through the twentieth century as a way of exploring an alternative history of architecture.

Historiography of architecture: historians and their histories

This is by necessity an idiosyncratic list, and different writers will find another selection of historians and theorists make the point better, but the following selection of writers represents some of the scope of architectural history as a discipline, and is illustrative of some of its potentials. The aim of architectural history is not to produce a dry chronology of events in the order that they happened, but rather to discuss the significance of these prior examples to the practice of architecture today. From the outset it is impossible – and perhaps undesirable – to disentangle the architectural historians from theorists and the practitioners from the academics: each has a valuable viewpoint on the grand narrative of architecture, and it is this notion of a story that might prove most instructive.

A classic example of storytelling is the great Japanese film-maker Akira Kurosawa's *Rashomon* (1950), based on two short stories by Ryunosuke Akutagawa.[1] The film was hugely influential in its narrative structure – particularly on later Hollywood courtroom dramas – as it depicts a murder observed by several witnesses and the subsequent trial. Each of the witnesses describes the event in completely different ways, each of which is true *from a certain point of view*, and these interpretations are played out on the screen for comparison.

In the same way, the historical record is available for interpretation by architectural historians and, to some extent, every architect is part historian in the same way that they are part theorist, part engineer, part designer, part entrepreneur.

The writers detailed on the following pages represent a range of opinions and approaches to architectural history. This is an operative history: one that affords some action, as every context that an architect will work in will have some social, cultural, economic and political aspect to which they must respond.

Manfredo Tafuri

The aim of Manfredo Tafuri's history is an examination of historical processes and how they operate to *produce* architecture.[2] This viewpoint allows him to see historical precedent in the influences forming architecture rather than simply as models to be copied. This distinction allows Tafuri's histories to see contemporary architecture as being formed and informed by similar processes: the importance of patronage and economic activity to architecture are not to be underestimated, but this does not produce an architectural history that is dry and procedural, but rather one that is informed by a wide range of influences, all contributing to a broader context.

The concept of an *operative* history is something directly refuted by Tafuri in his works, but he is writing against a context of postmodernism in architecture, where decorative forms would often be cited in structures and applied in an ironic or often pastiche fashion. The operative nature of architectural history does not have to be quite so didactic, but can be suggestive of how architects can act now, with some reference to the past.

Tafuri's project to uncover the underlying dynamics of architectural production takes a broad approach, and is tackled in his work on Renaissance architecture in Italy. In his foreword to the work, K. Michael Hays writes of Tafuri that:

Above: Utopian architecture in Kisho Kurokawa's Nakagin Capsule Tower.

Below: The megastructural impulse that followed the capsule in Japanese architecture, here the Kyoto International Conference Center by Sachio Otani.

> he wrote history to construct the laws of historical dynamics that govern systemic changes in social formations and cultural practices. Architecture is the primary exhibit in this great narrative because architecture is the most complexly contested and negotiated of all cultural production.[3]

Tafuri's studies include an examination of the concept of Utopia through the ages in which the concept is unpacked with reference to capitalist development. Rather than an unfixed concept that we all have reference to, Utopia is a process and an ideology: it is not a neutral concept, but one borne first of Enlightenment rationalism, furthered by Industrial Revolution positivism and developed through to the ideological in the twentieth century.

Tafuri challenges commonplace and accepted terminology, a rhetorical device that is valuable for a deeper understanding of concepts you are antagonistic towards, or even in some agreement with: it is your duty as an informed practitioner of architecture to think a little more about the terms of your debate, and Tafuri encourages this.

The eventual trajectory of the Japanese architectural movement Metabolism was to look to precedents such as Italian hill towns. Kurokawa brought this concept to the site of Hillside Terrace in Daikanyama, Tokyo, which he was able to develop over the course of two decades.

We might reasonably assume a term such as 'Utopia' to be both universally positive and also to exist outside history. This is in part down to the great efforts of Utopian thinkers to entrench the idea in this way, but its meaning is more specific and contested than it might first appear.

Utopianism has reference, knowingly or otherwise, to the origins of the term in Thomas More's novella *Utopia*, in which a speculation on the nature and organization of human society is explored.[4] Utopia, simply put, is often taken to mean an ideal place, but originally this term meant 'no-place' or 'any-place'. Utopia, in More's text, is an unfamiliar and disturbing place, but this placeless quality recurs in Utopian architecture: it is bereft of context, of site, of location. This can be rendered through devices of stretching the scheme across an entire territory, as in the case of Superstudio, or by having the city walk, as Archigram would have it – both radical 1960s architectural groups. The Utopian impulse is fundamentally anti-contextual, however, and Tafuri finds fault with this significant detail and believes it to be at the root of the eventual collapse of such well-meaning movements.

One of Tafuri's key findings is that architecture 'attempted to solve problems beyond the scope of the discipline', as described by Kate Nesbitt in her introduction to an extract from his *Architecture and Utopia*.[5] Tafuri is a difficult and complex writer, however, and others provide much more accessible variations on his thinking.

Colin Rowe

Colin Rowe's histories take a substantially different approach, but also with regard for the context of postwar modernism and the issues that rapid redevelopment and rebuilding raised in our cities.[6] Rowe was a committed architectural educator, and his interest in such form-based analysis reinforces that his is a history embedded wholly in the discipline of architecture.

Rowe's two most famous works – the book *Collage City*, co-authored with Fred Koetter, and the essay 'The Mathematics of the Ideal Villa' – both represent Rowe's fascination for the form taken by architecture.

Given their development over a long period, the cities of London and Edinburgh could be considered to be good examples of Rowe and Koetter's 'collage cities', in which history is often respected and built upon, resulting in coherent but differentiated urban form.

In *Collage City*, we see continuous use of the figure-ground plan, a deceptively simple tool for urban analysis (with its origins in Giambattista Nolli's 1748 plan of Rome), where buildings are rendered as a shaded figure, revealing the ground of the city, the paving, streets and public squares as white paper, or ground. Through this analysis, the ratio of figure to ground can be compared between one time and another, one city to another, revealing the ways in which modernism radically altered this relationship of built space to unbuilt: something that Rowe stresses has a disastrous outcome for the built environment.

Rowe is not absolutist, however, and moderates his diagnosis for solving this observed problem. Indeed, he argues that the problem arose due to the same Utopian thinking criticized by Tafuri, but that an approach where such admittedly more egalitarian and democratic architectures are accommodated alongside the old in a manner of a collage with all its connotations of unexpected juxtaposition could be a viable solution.

Rowe contends that there is an ethical aspect to architecture, and that modernism did a great deal of good along with its more destructive aspects. He stresses that we can have both extremes of the dichotomies of order/disorder; and that the key is co-existence rather than the existence of a single correct answer.

In 'The Mathematics of the Ideal Villa', Rowe examines the role of geometry in architecture through a series of case studies, notably Palladio's Villa Foscari (also known as the Malcontenta) and Le Corbusier's Villa Stein (or Villa Garches). Through this close analysis, Rowe argues that Corbusier's claims for a *New Architecture* were firmly grounded in a detailed understanding of his predecessors, in contrast to modernism's claims of a rupture with the past.

Robin Evans

This focus on representation is taken even further in the work of Robin Evans, who had an interest in the practices of drawing used by architects. The reason for this was an understanding of the process of making a drawing as an important scaffold for the thinking process used in designing; the idea of drawing as a presentation of ideas already perfected within the mind.

Evans presents these ideas in a concise form in *Translations from Drawing to Building*, with an essay titled 'The Developed Surface, an Enquiry into the Brief Life of an Eighteenth-Century Drawing Technique'.[7] This essay considers a curiosity, a curate's egg of a drawing convention, called a section – but distinctive from the usage we now have for this as a contraction of the cross-section. The section described here is a plan with each of the interior walls folded down and presented in elevation, aligned with the appropriate plan edge.

What is interesting is that this tells us a great deal about the focus of the designers of the time: on the interior space, the detailed mouldings of wall panelling and plastering, placement of furniture, and proportioning systems. The reasons why this was superseded by the conventional cross-section are investigated, but Evans gives us an architectural history that focuses not only on the making of the drawing, but also one that looks at the closed avenues, the practices that did not survive, but that reveal a great deal about the dominant thinking in that time and place.

It is instructive to consider the rapid changes taking place in architectural representation today, with the relatively recent reduction in use of the mechanical draughting table with parallel motion, T-square, pencils and inks. Packages and applications for CAD have also developed relatively rapidly and will no doubt be superseded by another form of representation in due course.

There is much to learn from this abandoned representation: it has lessons for contemporary architects, not least that it identifies what the priorities of the designer are. What, then, are the priorities of the parametrically oriented architect working with Grasshopper, or BIM's influence via Revit, and are they more or less appropriate? The distance of historical context equips us to better critique our own practices. As Evans writes in *The Projective Cast*, in which he examines three distinctive geometries for architecture,

> The job of a foundation is to be as firm as a rock. It is supposed to be inert. Dead things are easier to handle than live ones; they may not be so interesting but they are less troublesome. From the point of view of the architect seeking firmness and stability, the best geometry is surely a dead geometry, and perhaps that, by and large, is what architecture is made with. What I mean by a dead geometry is an aspect of geometry no longer under development from within.[8]

In this work, developments in geometrical thinking and understanding are shown to be active in architectural production; deterministic rather than determined by the will of the architect. Understanding geometries as systems for understanding space is the key, and as soon as the problem is cast in this light, the direct relevance to architecture is apparent.

Joseph Rykwert

Joseph Rykwert is an influential architectural critic and historian who tackles the origin myth of architecture in the West. *On Adam's House in Paradise* develops an understanding based on the hold this notion of the 'original' hut structure has had on the architectural imagination throughout history.[9] This hut is the point where humanity moves from claiming shelter from conveniently formed natural features, and begins to deliberately manipulate the environment to provide shelter.

The aim of this origin seeking is not to find a single point from which all progress can be measured, however: Rykwert is looking to understand what is fundamental to the discipline of architecture – what are the most powerful concepts of dwelling that recur throughout the various intersecting histories of the world? Why, indeed, is it important to perceive origins at all? What are the claims made for this?

The most important claim made for the originating house is that, as it was the first, it was also the *correct* way for us to live: that it has some spiritual or moral authority. Rykwert is tracing the history of ideas that have influenced architecture – not the buildings or works in themselves, but the underlying belief systems that brought them into being. This is a significantly different project from the simple chronology and categorization of architecture into styles and movements; it is not the dry

Of course, the primitive hut typology is also found outside Europe. This affectation is found, for example, in Katsura Imperial Villa, a deliberate citing of peasant architecture.

work of art history in which the canon is established and works are assessed as being more or less representative of an individual's oeuvre. Thus, the idea of an original house is traced back to the oldest surviving written work about architecture – Vitruvius' *De Architectura*. The accounts of so-called primitive huts have a historical impulse behind them:

> The writers on architectural theory I have quoted in this essay acknowledged the relevance of the primitive hut directly or indirectly, since it has provided so many of them with a point of reference for all speculation on the essentials of building. These speculations intensify when the need is felt for a renewal of architecture. Nor is this interest limited to speculation: various theorists have attempted to reconstruct such a hut in three dimensions and show the 'natural' form of the building; natural, rational or divinely revealed according to their lights.[10]

Rykwert's concern is with what constitutes architecture at all. Other key titles include *The Dancing Column*, in which he investigates the metaphor of the human body in the Classical orders.[11] Such loaded symbolism allows an interpretation of architecture as having its roots in humanity, and if so, Rykwert poses the question of what the implications are of building in this manner. In a later work, *The Judicious Eye*, he considers the place of architecture as one of the visual arts; a convention that was only relatively recently overturned saw architecture grouped alongside painting and sculpture.[12] How can we define the discipline of architecture at all? Again, Rykwert does this by drawing from history, constructing a trajectory that sees architectural identity as contingent rather than fixed and final.

Nikolaus Pevsner

Pevsner is often referred to as a short-hand for the series of gazetteers he initiated under the title Buildings of England and published one county at a time. The series has been extended to include Buildings of Scotland, Buildings of Wales and Buildings of Ireland, as well as the

The colonnade at St Peter's in Rome demonstrates the importance of the column to Western architecture.

Pevsner City Guides. These are authoritative guides to the architecture of a given locale, most helpful as a starting point to your investigations of a given context.[13]

The sense of completeness of the series necessitates an approach reliant more on facts and detailed description than on a critical analysis or appraisal of the place of each building within the context of architectural history. This is not a failing, but rather a quality of the publications that must be accepted. The series continues to be updated today, under different authorship and editorship, but maintaining Pevsner's original format to a great degree.

Pevsner was, of course, a historian of some regard beyond this project, with major works including *An Outline of European Architecture* and *Visual Planning and the Picturesque*.[14] Pevsner belongs to the art-historical tradition, having first engaged in teaching as a lecturer in art history, seeing architectural history as a branch of this rather than a separate discipline. He famously and influentially stated that 'A bicycle shed is a building. Lincoln cathedral is a piece of architecture.'[15]

The implications of this pithy remark are significant: to determine what is within the scope of architecture is something that all architects will wrestle with at different points in their career. Is it possible to define what is relegated to building, and is it even a lesser category, or merely something that conforms to a different set of criteria?

This speaks to the larger question of the relevance of a piece of architecture: by determining it as a building, Pevsner is saying that there is nothing to learn from it, that it is not significant. The role of Pevsner's background as an art historian emerges in his elaboration of the distinction: 'The term architecture only applies to buildings designed with a view to aesthetic appeal.'[16]

This bias is interesting, and questionable. How many would agree with this and – if not – where would the line be drawn between a building and architecture? Does the bicycle shed become architecture as soon as we see the juxtaposition of a bike with protective ramshackle shack as something beautiful, even if accidental?

Case study: The architectural manifesto

This case study explores a very specific history of architecture: the documents of architectural intent produced by the avant garde in the twentieth century.[17] The progression from manifesto to agenda, then position statement and finally method represents the way in which the manifesto fell out of favour as overly didactic, but the rupture between alternating periods of classicism and romanticism and the modern period left a legacy of architects making statements with their works.

A broader history of the artistic manifesto is required before focusing on the many charters and documents produced by architects. This history of architecture asks you to take a position, to have an opinion, and to be prepared to defend it. Architecture here is more than merely *building*. These documents challenge architects to describe what their architecture is *about*.

The account that follows gives contradictory and conflicting accounts of architecture: sometimes directly and violently opposing; other times only after the implications and reasoning are interrogated more fully. A position may be political, based on an attitude towards the everyday social and economic facts of life; it might be aesthetic, a consideration of what form architecture should take; it might be a process, a practice, a way of doing architecture. It may be all of these things.

This is intended to be a strident and energetic history, contentious and argumentative, passionate and grounded in individual interpretations of the world around us. The focus here is on politics with a small 'p' – the quotidian engagement with the urban condition rather than party politics. You might align with the left or the right; you might disregard such twentieth-century oppositions, or be informed by them.

An agenda must be *knowing* and *knowledgeable*, relevant and achievable. It asks you to define the condition of the world and state your position regarding that condition. What can you do *as an architect*? What are the limits of architecture?

Anatomy of a manifesto
A public statement of intent.
A definition of a problem.
A proposition of a solution.
A means for producing it.

A manifesto is most often issued by a group rather than an individual, but at its most basic level, the etymology of manifesto is from the Latin *manifestum*, defined as making something clear, manifest or conspicuous. Typically, the manifesto has a political purpose, if broadly sketched, rather than a religious one. The use of manifestos in art and architecture reflected a shift towards the political nature of space concurrent with the emergence of modernism.

Defining a problem
What is wrong with the world? Manifestos place architects and artists in the context of the world as it is now. This is often defined as a problem in search of a solution. This might be something as straightforward as a lack of adequate and affordable housing. This leads manifestos in many divergent directions, however. It is not enough to state a problem: you must define your approach to solving the issue.

Defining your solution

How do you propose to solve the problem? What are the resources required, and how do you express your priorities?

Taking a position

Why have you chosen this solution?
Present a defence of your position.
What are you actually interested in?
What is important to you?
What are you about as an architect?
What would you like to change?
Who are you and why should we care too?
Why should we accept your impressing your will upon the world?

Manifesto: Agenda: Position: Method

Each of the movements and agendas in this case study were measured against the above matrix. This is intended as a way of understanding the content of each movement's statement. Is it expressed as all four simultaneously, or does the expression only cover two or three? As such, the four terms need a working definition.

Manifesto is understood to be the public declaration that someone outside the originating group might be able to pick up on and subscribe to. Manifestos should attract adherents, not remain relevant only to those who wrote them. The second is an *agenda*. This can be hidden or explicit, and refers to the wider goal of the manifesto. Does the statement contain a clearly described agenda, such as a political motive in favour of workers, promoting the early Communist ideals so popular with avant-garde art movements? This is often presented as self-evident, but a *position* might be taken to explain why this is important either politically or artistically. Commonplace statements in this regard position the statement as having a place in the world as it is rather than as a distinctive category of art objects or historically consistent architecture. This is the position of the statement: the explanation of why. Many manifestos skip this, being so passionately written as to see this as self-evident. Finally, to *method*: what are the means by which this is to be achieved? In the case of artistic examples, there might be a move towards photorealism or towards abstraction. In architecture, there might be a regard for materiality, modes of production, economics or other ways of achieving the effect. Many manifestos and position statements skip this, too, leaving it open to the interpretation of the adherent; similarly some methods are presented that are supposedly neutral towards the more political aspects of the statement.

Space limitations permit just one case to be discussed here, so it seemed appropriate to consider one of the most important architectural examples of our time: Le Corbusier's hugely influential *Towards a New Architecture*.[18]

Other examples considered included:

Le Corbusier's Modulor: Proportioning system as manifesto.

De Stijl: Art becomes life, erasing distinctions between the arts and between life and art.

Athens Charter: Laying the groundwork for CIAM and the International Style.

Superstudio: The continuous monument – manifesto as satire, proposition as critique.

Archigram: Further prototypes, science-fiction positivism in architecture.

Cedric Price: Questioning the fundamental nature of architecture. What is it for?

Constant and the Situationist International: Radical politics and architecture.

Le Corbusier and the prototype

Manifesto: Agenda: Position: Method

A key document of the modern movement, *Towards a New Architecture* set Le Corbusier's theory of architecture in straightforward terms, much of which is canonical to the development of modernist architecture. The key strategy used within the text is of interest in and of itself, however, as it is one with both a long history and a persisting utility for today's architecture. The model or prototype is a useful and pragmatic way to understand and develop architecture.

Corbusier begins with an account of the importance of industrial architecture, as attractive as it is utilitarian and without decorative embellishments: this is building without frivolity. A certain nobility is suggested for lock gates in docks, grain silos, factory spaces and warehouses. This is an aspirational model: Corbusier wishes his architecture to have this same simplicity and noble translation of function into form, where sculptural qualities are derived from necessity.

The thesis is divided into three 'reminders' for architects:
Mass
Surface
Plan

This new architecture proposed by Corbusier is, then, to be defined in terms of three factors. These are more than simple: they are so fundamental to architecture that it is impossible to think of architecture without reference to them. Can there be any architecture without mass? Is it possible to have an architecture without surface? Is the absence of plan conceivable?

Mass is the first reminder, suggesting that architects have forgotten this as a concept. This is another strategy of the manifesto: to reinstate some condition that has been lost to us. The reminders proposed by Corbusier simultaneously place his 'new' architecture in a historical context and against it.

Below: This silo in Düsseldorf shows some of the hallmarks of mass, as discussed by Corbusier in his manifesto.

Mass is represented by the grain elevator – examples of enormous monolithic industrial buildings, often with curved forms; a series of tall cylinders that clash with blocky elements and exposed structure. The pure form of the massive brick edifice is what interests Corbusier here, as a prototype of his concept of mass.

Mass has an implication of weighty, plastic (in the sense that sculpture is often described as a plastic art, rather than the manufactured petrochemical substance) form that is revealed by the play of light over it. There is a relationship between lighting conditions, viewing conditions and geometries that excites the eye. There is a directness in Corbusier's prototype here: scale is certainly also a factor in the heroism of such structures, but these are unapologetic buildings, prefiguring the brutalist architecture that was to follow later in the modernist discourse.

Surface is similarly geometrical to Corbusier. He develops a notion of 'directing and generating lines'[19] and, conceding an interesting nod to the individuality of a piece of architecture residing in its surface,

Below: The celebration of industrial architecture continues in buildings such as the Red Dot Design Museum, located in a disused colliery on the Zollverein Coal Mine Industrial Complex in Germany. This gallery by Foster + Partners arranges design classics against the backdrop of a rusting, abandoned factory.

something dangerously close to ornament that other modernists (see Adolf Loos on *Ornament and Crime*, for example) would have rejected roundly.[20] The factory building returns, but such a mundane building is compared to the Renaissance exemplar of Bramante in what would have been heretical to some at the time.

There is some fantastic terminology in the text here: the idea of an 'accusing line' is a phrase that indicates some of the poetry of Corbusier among the hard-headed functionalism. What does a line accuse? What crimes might it be revealing?

Third of this triumvirate is plan, conceptualized as 'the generator'.[21] Poetry is firmly embedded in Corbusier's thinking, alongside order, structure and law. Plan is the root of sensation: of perceptual experience. This is an enormously important statement, one worthy of breaking down. As a set of spatial relations, plan form is more than a visual representation, but an arrangement and setting into sequence of experience. Certain sequences are permissible within a plan, others are no longer available to us. The plan controls what we see through that frame; what we hear and how; what we smell, taste and feel: always *when*.

Corbusier's exemplars here are notably classical – the Acropolis, Santa Sophia – but by association he is looking to suggest these plans as something separate from the architectural styles they represent: 'The plan carries in itself the very essence of sensation.'[22]

Le Corbusier's repetition of this phrase carries the weight of a mantra. He goes on, after citing these antique examples, to note that plan has been neglected for the last 100 years: again the tactic of simultaneously contextualizing within and rejecting outright his immediate history. The way forward is to be grounded in necessity, statistics, calculation and geometry.

The next section takes three explicitly contemporary prototypes that represent the cutting edge of 1920s technology under the title 'Eyes That Do Not See'.[23] This tirade against style is really against the prevailing Beaux-Arts style of the earlier period, derived from classicism and romanticism rather freely, and built according to patterns published in books, established or tried-and-tested plans, and sets of detailing: standardized responses realized through largely handmade craftsmanship. Corbusier was set against the *parti* here, and sought to establish his own systems appropriate to his epoch – the industrialized production of architecture.[24]

We are presented with three aspirations here:
The Ocean Liner
The Automobile
The Aeroplane

This notion of the correct statement of problems has a common root with philosophy prevalent at the time, particularly that of Henri Bergson. Bergson offers many insights into the nature of problem-solving. In stating a problem correctly, he holds that a scientific or speculative problem may be solved, as the solution to such problems is possible, or inherent in its correct statement. We are reminded that 'the possible is only the real with the addition of an act of mind that throws its image back into the past, once it has been enacted'.[25]

> We imagine that everything that occurs could have been foreseen by any sufficiently informed mind, and that, in the form of an idea, it was then pre-existent to its realization; an absurd conception in the case of a work of art, for from the moment that the musician has the precise and complete idea of the symphony he means to compose, his symphony is done.[26]

It is in this respect that Bergson finds more interest: the creative problem, which resists such possibility, forces us into a solution that relies upon duration. That is to say, a process must be engaged with over a period of time.

'The house is a machine for living in.'[27]

The above quote constitutes the most famous dictum of Corbusier's work. This is the operation by which he establishes his agenda: the prototype is adapted, considering the terms on which it can be adopted by architecture. We have three feats of engineering that can be considered as a category – as very successful forms of machine. This commonality allows Corbusier, in his manifesto-forming practice, to identify a common root to all three prototypes: as machines. What kind of machine might architecture be in this case? A machine *for living in* is the answer.

Corbusier's process is interpretation of the prototype: the streamlined tactility of an ocean liner's fittings, the engineered precision part-making of automobile production lines, and the extreme form-giving conditions required to take an aeroplane into the air. These are modern examples that, at each scale of the design, from engineering down to fixtures and fittings, are conceived as complete works, and formed by or conforming to a specified set of parameters. This was the model Corbusier expected architecture to follow.

The aim of a study like this one is to expose the manifesto's historical operation as a process contingent upon the concerns of the time, and one that continues to inform architects today. Today's terms of reference are more often to do with sustainability and digital design, but these are no less polemic than the intervention of the modernists. An understanding of the historical manifesto makes it possible to work in a more informed way with such documents as they are produced today.

Chapter 11:
The politics of space

That space has a political aspect might, at first glance, appear to be either perfectly natural or absolutely absurd. In terms of the politics of the built environment, one thinker is commonly understood to form a basis for discussion: the sociologist Henri Lefebvre.

The key concept in Lefebvre's thinking on the city is the *right to the city*: that is, the degree to which any member of society can access what the city has to offer.[1] This underlines one of the most important disciplines contributing to architecture: an understanding of the politics of space and the implications of power relations in space.

Lefebvre's approach complicates the view of the city by considering the mechanisms by which it is established largely for the good of vested interests, be these the Church or the nobility in historical contexts, or commercial processes of commodification in the case of the contemporary. Buildings can be said to exert power over people. Such excessive agency can serve a valid purpose, where the correct functioning of a space requires certain forms of behaviour in order to function. Examples might be libraries, courts of law or lecture halls. When such constraints begin to expand outside of this realm, however, problems begin to emerge.

Recent events demonstrate the simple power of presence in a place: in the Arab Spring, the Occupy movement, and the long tradition of taking to the streets to protest. The simple fact of presence in a space is significant politically, particularly when this goes against the needs and desires of established authority, be that a regime or an economic structure.

There are ethical implications to our political engagements with space. Gated communities create enclaves of limited diversity, shopping malls replace truly public space with controlled environments where the

Page 140: The Reichstag,
New German Parliament
Building, Berlin. Norman
Foster, 1992-1999.

only permissible activity is consumption. Rather than employ a single methodology, politically engaged research can take advantage of a range or approaches, but the effects of the control that governance, finance and commerce have on the city is fertile ground for research in architecture.

This chapter concludes by drawing on work conducted by the 'Cultures of Legibility' research project, which looked at the city of Jakarta, Indonesia, and the everyday experience of people there.

Politics and the language of architecture

Writing in 'Politics and the English Language' in 1946, the essayist George Orwell writes:

> In our age there is no such thing as 'keeping out of politics'. All issues are political issues, and politics itself is a mass of lies, evasions, folly, hatred, and schizophrenia.[2]

By extension, we can argue that there is no such thing as an apolitical act, and no architecture that is beyond the politics of the day. Architecture exists within a wide network of interests, from individual clients and building users through to local planning control and governmental structures, through to global finance and commodities markets determining the costs of materials, labour and land.

Street art in New York. Simple acts can appropriate the city away from vested interests, and one such challenge to property is the preponderance of graffiti art.

The idea of the political act in architecture can extend beyond what is permissible in the normative models of architectural practice, and challenges architects to consider what alternative systems are possible, and to what extent a building conforms to the strictures of the dominant paradigm. Simply put, politics can't be avoided in the most innocent act as speaking, so a complex, multifaceted activity such as architectural design and construction is a deeply entrenched political endeavour.

As with other essays, Orwell equips the reader with some things to avoid in order to rehabilitate the English language. These could serve architects and researchers equally well:

Never use a metaphor, simile, or other figure of speech which you are used to seeing in print. Of course, this is somewhat provocative (and rightly so) in terms of conservationist and historicist trends in architecture, but perhaps prompts careful consideration when referencing older forms of building: what is suggested by that structural element, what associations does it have to religion or power that you would rather not associate with? The caryatid is a good case here. These female statues, which adorn Classical architecture, are associated with the expression of wealth, and a representation of slave ownership. The architect might very well reinterpret the caryatid in contemporary architecture, but must be mindful of the legacy of such figures. Orwell's original point remains within architectural writing practices as well. Well-worn phrases and clichés accumulate so many meanings over time as to become vague, while a novel comparison or metaphor refreshes language and allows something new to be said.

Never use a long word where a short one will do. Many writers have a tendency to overcomplicate matters and to use elaborate language in order to give an air of authority to their research or practice. While precision often demands certain terminology, it remains best practice to speak and write plainly. When considering theory, architects can fall into the trap of appropriating jargon from other disciplines – notably philosophy – and entering into word games that end up obscuring rather than revealing meaning. This runs absolutely counter to the aim of the exercise. Similarly, in design, such elaborations are associated with movements such as the Baroque and Rococo, which, it is worth remembering, had an explicit ideological and political purpose: the Counter-Reformation. It is essential that we understand the implications of such elaborate language as a form of enchantment.

If it is possible to cut a word out, always cut it out. A more extreme example of the above is to ask whether something is necessary at all. This fuller form of editing asks for an economy and efficiency in building or in writing: is the word or feature an embellishment designed to generate a particular aura, or is it actually useful to building users or readers? Does it function or communicate, or is it redundant? The redundancy of this aesthetic enthusiasm does say something, and you want to avoid saying inadvertently something that you do not actually mean.

Never use the passive when you can use the active. Speaking of language again, this asks for a directness, clarity and obviousness of means. This can also refer to research and architectural design itself. When writing on architecture, it can be more comfortable to remain indirect to the point of saying nothing. This is a trap, possibly one of mindfulness where there is an intention of fairness and even-handedness, but remember that once all of your data, evidence and theory has been considered, the point is to say *something*. The referencing and literature backed up by your fieldwork and findings gives you permission to say something about the world, but careful research can often paralyse the researcher into timidity.

Never use a foreign phrase, a scientific word, or a jargon word if you can think of an everyday English equivalent. Orwell's concern for the English language is not reductive, but a further extension of his principal idea: you must write straightforwardly, and avoid elaborate phrases that are a kind of disguise or attempt to dazzle the reader. Validating one's research through extensive use of jargon is lazy, and often an indication that the practical application of the research to everyday life has not been thought through.

Break any of these rules sooner than say anything outright barbarous. As with all things, a get-out clause can be useful, and Orwell recognizes that any guidance can result in abuses – or, barbarous statements. The rules are not a formula for the production of politically intelligent debate, after all, and barbarous ideas can still be presented in plain, straightforward language (although Orwell's point throughout the essay is that euphemism and misdirection are used to disguise truly barbaric acts).

The point of these strictures on language is to encourage a consideration of what is being said politically, whether plainly in written research, or by extension, in the 'language' of architecture. This is a contestable idea, but one that will serve you well: buildings can have meanings, and your choices on how to build do say something of that intention.

Below: Expressions of power in architecture: (a) the Palace of Westminster; (b) the Reichstag in Berlin, decontextualized after international competition by Norman Foster; (c) Lunar House in Croydon (an immigration processing centre); and (d) the new Seoul City Hall by iArc Architects, dominating the old Japanese colonial administration headquarters.

a

b

c

d

The right to the city

Henri Lefebvre[3] famously introduced the ideas of the *right to the city* (later adopted and elaborated by theorists including David Harvey[4]) and the *social production of space* into architectural thinking. Lefebvre's works often address architecture and urbanism directly, discussing the ways in which the built environment operates to alienate people. This key process of alienation is a political one, and Lefebvre uses this to complicate and problematize our relationship with everyday life. This idea of the everyday is crucial to architecture (although the architectural press might prefer to discuss the spectacular and the extraordinary), which both deals with the everyday and, to an extent, channels and controls the quotidian stuff of life. This comes from a context of the development of Marxist thought in France, moving beyond a presumed return to the critique of the bourgeois against a context of extreme political drama in the twentieth century.[5]

> The remarkable way in which modern techniques have penetrated everyday life has thus introduced into this backward sector *the uneven development* which characterizes every aspect of our era. Manifestations of the brilliant advances in the 'ideal home' constitute sociological facts of the first importance, but they must not be allowed to conceal the contradictory character of the real social process beneath an accumulation of technological detail.[6]

Lefebvre gives examples of persuasive hairdressers using the machinery of fashion magazines and celebrity culture to justify their desire to cut hair in a particular fashion, or the presence of new forms of kitchen even to the detriment of other aspects of life: new *social needs* that usurp the real necessities of life and often eclipse them. The things we take for granted are social processes, and in need of critique.

With regards to the production of space, Lefebvre underlines the aspect of *production*:

> There is nothing, in history or in society, which does not have to be achieved and produced. 'Nature' itself, as apprehended in social life by the sense organs, has been modified and therefore in a sense produced. Human beings have produced juridical, political, religious, artistic and philosophical forms. The production in the broad sense of the term embraces a multiplicity of works and a great diversity of forms, even forms that do not bear the stamp of the producer or of the production process.[7]

The process of this production is a social one, a collaborative one, a relational one. It is something that is mediated through relationships and our engagement with one another, standing in opposition to the Cartesian idea of space as an abstract concept – a set of coordinates and geometries.

This culminates in Lefebvre's most influential idea: that of the right to the city, whereby the city is seen as a resource and set of opportunities to which we all, as citizens, have a right. Expressing it in these absolute terms is interesting, as it presents the city as a socially produced space once again, and demonstrates that there is a process by which people are prevented from taking advantage of it and participating in it.

Society of the spectacle

A counterpoint to Lefebvre's thinking is Guy Debord's important essay *The Society of the Spectacle*. Dealing with many of the same issues, the critique is subtly different, arguing that the spectacular nature of the contemporary urban environment is problematic in itself, and open to subversion through simple means, such as the alternative modes of using or occupying the city by walking in ways such as those suggested by the Situationist *dérive*, or *drift*.

Below: Appropriation of space can be both positive and negative, such as the everyday occupation of the plaza in front of Mies van der Rohe's Seagram Building, or this film crew's claim over a New York street, commoditizing the space and denying regular users some of their rights. Similarly, the takeover of Edinburgh for its festival every August shows how appropriation can be simultaneously counter-cultural and mainstream, often to the chagrin of city residents.

> The capitalist production system has unified space, breaking down the boundaries between one society and the next. This unification is also a process, at once extensive and intensive, of *trivialization*.[8]

The Society of the Spectacle is a polemic that has proven influential in architectural thinking, even if it is not directly applicable. Like many such texts, it asks the right questions, but does not prescribe what action the architect ought to take. Indeed, the works of the architect most closely associated with the Situationists (who went by the

singular name of Constant), with whom Debord was associated, were monolithic super-modernist Utopias that bear a tangential relationship to the idea of taking the city back through alternative occupation and dwelling patterns.[9]

Debord's critique of urbanism as a movement politicizes the entire activity of urban design and architecture.

> In all previous periods, architectural innovation served the ruling class exclusively; now for the first time there is such a thing as a new architecture specifically for the poor. Both formal poverty and the immense extension of this new experience in housing are the result of its *mass* character, dictated at once by its ultimate ends and by the modern conditions of construction. At the core of these conditions we naturally find an *authoritarian decision-making process* that abstractly develops any environment into an environment of abstraction.[10]

This is similar to Lefebvre's process of *alienation*, whereby connections between everyday life and the poetic or spiritual life are severed. Many writers of this period struggled with the idea of abstracted, geometric space and how it integrates with occupied space often described as *place*. These stances challenge you to consider the nature of the discipline and how it acts upon people. What is the political result of architecture? Can this be subverted by occupying space differently?

The Parisian arcades, or passages, as the prototype of spectacle in space described by Debord.

Top left and right: Political architecture often has recourse to the concept of Utopia, which is frequently attempted and discussed. Some alternative approaches include Moshe Safdie's Habitat 67, which uses self-similar units arranged in unique ways, and the technological Utopia of Richard Rogers' high-tech Lloyd's of London building.

Centre and bottom: The Matadero in Madrid is an attempt to create a flexible art space and enterprise incubator for the people of Madrid rather than a tourist designation. It includes music rehearsal and production facilities, a cinema, gallery, archive, and a public square with movable units for shade, seating and contemplation.

Case study: 'Cultures of Legibility'

The 'Cultures of Legibility' research project was a collaboration between the University of Edinburgh and the National University of Indonesia under the leadership of Professor Stephen Cairns. It sought to understand the city of Jakarta through a series of interviews and mapping techniques. Much of the politics of this project is in the sense of the everyday, recalling Lefebvre's focus on this as a critique. One of the key contributions of the project was to consider the importance of mapping the city in a way that responded to the lives of a wide variety of residents.

The project takes a transect through the west of the city, which includes a variety of different conditions, including well-heeled residential complexes, informal *kampung* settlements, golf clubs, shopping malls, technology parks, rice fields and an international airport.

A series of interviews were conducted by Masters students at the National University of Indonesia. The first, detailed interview method involved a video interview and mental mapping exercise that drew on Peter Gould and Rodney White, as well as Kevin Lynch, for the methodology.[11] The second interview method was a wider survey, which was completed through a tightly controlled questionnaire. The detailed interviews yielded a range of different understandings of the city, from the taxi drivers who knew a vast array of routes through the city, to the village elder who rarely left the orbit of his own dwelling. In between these poles were people who had habitual routes to other parts of the city.

The methods presented in Lynch's seminal *Image of the City* were challenged by the city of Jakarta. The original text investigated a number of North American cities – most notably Boston – that could be understood in terms of their visual image, with clearly identified neighbourhoods, a hierarchy of routes through the city, and a wealth of public space to serve as nodes. The hypothesis of the research project was that Lynch's model of *imageability* breaks down when presented with the rapidly urbanizing condition of Jakarta. The case was somewhat more complicated than this, and resulted in a refinement and modification rather than an outright rejection of Lynch's method.

By transcribing the mental maps of our respondents into Lynch's symbolism, it became clear that there were equivalents to aspects such as *landmarks* that, in the original system, are largely visual items, but that can make their presence felt in other ways. One of the most interesting variations was the *temporality* of a landmark. Certain events such as a traffic jam or illegal road race, both of which occurred frequently, were significant enough to constitute landmarks. These sites were used to navigate *even when the event that granted them this significance was not happening*. Their presence was socially produced rather than visible

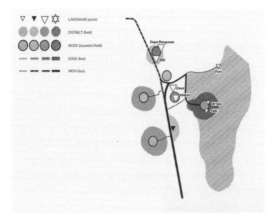
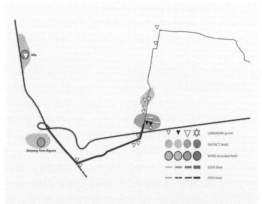

Above: Redrawn and coded mental maps of individual respondents.

Right: Photographs depicting the wide variety of conditions found in the chosen transect through the city of Jakarta.

to the eye, so the structure of navigation within Jakarta was substantially different to that which is found in Boston.

The implications of the study are not unlike early experiments in documentary film-making, where producers such as John Grierson would try to give voice to the workers in British industry by telling their stories on film, or allowing them to appear and tell their own stories.[12] This is a way of making populations present to research, and asking them directly what their experience of space is. Working with this material gives a substantially more nuanced version of the city than official planning bodies provide, as it accounts for the ad hoc, the illegal, the illicit, the transgressive uses of space – many of which are legitimate opportunities for residents of the city, who arguably have a greater right to the space than the gentrification of walled compounds and golf clubs.

Architectural research can therefore have a more explicit agenda, such as the protection of a community asset, assessing the design needs and preferences of a marginalized group of people, or making proposals that learn from ad hoc and informal architectures that are explicitly socially produced.

The final map, collating each of the 100 respondents' experiences of the city.

TOMATO
SOUP
"TRADEMARKS, CAMPBELL SOUP COMPANY. ALL RIGHTS RESERVED."

Chapter 12:
Philosophy, phenomenology and the experience of space

One of the most pertinent forms of philosophical enquiry to architecture is phenomenology, which explores the fundamental idea of being. Two branches of this philosophy have been fruitful: the relationship between being and dwelling explored by Martin Heidegger, and the phenomenology of perception described by Maurice Merleau-Ponty.

This chapter, in describing how to work with such theories, is intended as an example of how to apply philosophical concepts to architecture. This has been a rich vein for research for some time, and such theories can be used to frame your research in a rigorous, thoughtful manner. The chapter concludes with some of my own work on *sensory urbanism* and *sensory notation*, which was strongly influenced by phenomenology.

Applications of philosophy to architecture

There is a long history of philosophy's influence over architecture, one that continues to this day. As the basis for theory in architecture, philosophy represents a coherent systematization of thinking that tends towards the fundamental questions of life, often to the point of abstracting the query from concrete examples. This, however, is where architectural theory becomes useful, as it interprets and addresses such concerns to those of the built environment.

Several key theories are perennially important to architectural debates, and one of the benefits of philosophy is that it rarely dates: there is always a new application or inflection that can be made of a much older theory, often stretching back as far as antiquity.

Care must be taken, though, to avoid the tendency for obscurity, where arguments become self-referential and entirely enclosed. This defeats the point of philosophical enquiry in architecture, becoming a logical game or exercise of pure rhetoric rather than something that actually allows for new understandings of existing buildings, or innovations in their design.

Two models for the interaction of the two fields of interest are clear: philosophy that informs our discussion of architecture and the work of architects and philosophies that inform the design of the buildings in the first instance. Additionally, philosophy might be derived from architecture, as a variation of the relationship between philosophy and extant works of architecture. This third option is rarer, however.

Linguistic analogies in architecture

Language has long held a fascination for philosophy, and for some time in the twentieth century, semiotic theory held sway among architects keen to explore the idea that architecture can convey meaning. One of the most engaging versions of this theory can be found in Robert Venturi, Denise Scott Brown and Steven Izenour's seminal work, *Learning from Las Vegas*,[1] In this text, it is argued that architecture, so long dismissive of commercial architecture such as the Las Vegas strip, should in fact turn its attention to the directness with which it communicates.

Page 152 and below: Here is an example that complicates the model of the Duck and Decorated Shed, the Royal Scottish Academy in Edinburgh, preparing for an Andy Warhol exhibition.

In charting the structures of the strip and other vernacular American architecture, the authors identify two key operations: the Duck and the Decorated Shed. The Duck is named after a small roadside establishment selling duck meat and duck eggs in Long Island, New York. The connection is clear: this thing that resembles a duck also provides you with cooked duck. Venturi *et al* further claim that all buildings with unnecessary formal flourishes, where the heavy symbolism overpowers other aspects of the design, can be categorized as Ducks. Playing with this absurdity is a deliberate part of the argument, and the authors claim that the relationship of building (schematic house) to sign (word) to symbol (eye) can be expressed as a continuum of possibilities, including bazaars, medieval streets, cathedrals and triumphal arches. The critique and understanding of semiotics make odd bedfellows in architecture, forcing you to think about the buildings concerned in completely different terms.

Duck: Building as sign
'Where the architectural systems of space, structure and program are submerged and distorted by an overall symbolic form.'[2]

Decorated Shed: Big sign, little building
'Where systems of space and structure are directly at the service of program, and ornament is applied independently of them.'[3]

The critique is pursued through photographs, maps, drawings and diagrams that catalogue the Las Vegas strip, mapping the words visible from the highway, the relationship between built space and car parking, levels of illumination and more. This search for meaning results in an alternative *order*, harking back to Classical proportioning systems:

> the order of the Strip *includes*; it includes at all levels, from the mixture of seemingly incongruous land uses to the mixture of seemingly incongruous advertising media plus a system of neo-Organic or neo-Wrightian restaurant motifs in Walnut Formica. It is not an order dominated by the expert and made easy for the eye. The moving eye in the moving body must work to pick out and interpret a variety of changing, juxtaposed orders, like the shifting configurations of a Victor Vesely painting.[4]

We can see the results of this thinking in Venturi and Scott Brown's subsequent architecture, where the early postmodernist movement in architecture recognized the need for architecture to carry meaning. This was achieved through various means, including historical quotation, which was sometimes over-scaled or tongue in cheek, and at other times more subtle and considered, but the accusation of irony haunts the movement, an often unfair critique that positions the architects involved as being incapable of genuine use of historical motifs and forms.

In his ongoing project to investigate the notion of programme and function in architecture, defining them as creative acts in themselves, Bernard Tschumi's oeuvre as an architectural theorist is of interest.

Complications such as Herzog & De Meuron's intervention in an old building for the CaixaForum in Madrid show some of the potential and complexity of linguistic analogies in architecture.

When confronted with an artistic program, an architect may either:

a. Design a masterly construction, an inspired architectural gesture
(a composition)
b. Take what exists, fill in the gaps, complete the text, scribble in
the margins (a complement)
c. Deconstruct what exists by critically analyzing the historical
layers that preceded it, even adding other layers derived from
elsewhere—from other cities, other parks (a palimpsest)
d. Search for an intermediary—an abstract system to mediate
between the site (as well as all given constraints) and some other
concept, beyond city or program (a mediation).[5]

Bernard Tschumi's La Villette
project in Paris.

In many ways the actual *sign* can be regarded as arbitrary: it can be
anything that carries any given meaning, so long as it communicates by
an agreed system. The bare bones of Saussurian semiology are as follows,
depicting the way that communication relies upon the correspondence
of signifier with signified – we must agree that a given word denotes this
particular thing:

Signified: The thing itself – the object or concept that is being
communicated.
Signifier: The means of the communication, be that a word or a
visual symbol.
Sign: The combination of the signifier and the signified is required to
produce a sign. This represents a communication that is successful
– the signifier corresponds to the signified thing in the mind of the
receiver of a message.

Tschumi, however, partly in response to writers such as Derrida, is
encouraged to play further with this idea of meaning and communication
in architecture. Regarding his park at La Villette in Paris, his first major
commission, Tschumi writes:

La Villette, then, aims at an architecture that *means nothing*, an
architecture of the signifier rather than the signified—one that is
pure trace or play of language ... the effect of refusing fixity is not
insignificance but semantic plurality.[6]

In this way, Tschumi is developing a deconstructivist architecture, where
meaning is far from absolute, but open and plural. This finds resonance
with writers such as Roland Barthes and Umberto Eco, who were moving
away from the stability of older models of meaning and transmission, and
towards more contingent and variable ideas. Tschumi's innovation is to move
beyond this 'death of the author' thesis towards deliberate exploitation of
the open work: an architecture that resists clarity of meaning.

Dwelling and being-in-space

The philosophy of Martin Heidegger holds a perennial interest for architects. As a philosopher who considered the importance of dwelling, and interactions between people and tools or technology, he contributes to a body of work that speaks – often directly – to architecture.[7]

Heidegger famously wrote in an isolated forest hut, and this site has become emblematic of his thinking as well as providing the context for his thinking. It is consistent with Heidegger's philosophy that the context within which we think and write is of great importance, and that this hut, with its forest and mountain aspect, modest in scale and ambition, enabled Heidegger the clarity of mind to think about the world. This inextricability between the location and the thought is explored rigorously by architectural theorist Adam Sharr.[8]

A key Heidegger text is 'Building Dwelling Thinking'.[9] Here, reference is made to the *fourfold* of Earth, Sky, Mortals and Divinities. This is a complex concept, but the *fourfold* basically represent the aspects of the world that Heidegger considers essential for thought.

Heidegger expresses something primal and fundamental about dwelling, which extends its meaning beyond merely residing in a place and towards concepts of comfort and homeliness, as well as the temporality of maintaining a home: this is not a static state, but one that must be constantly kept up through various practices. Heidegger's research question in the lecture then comes into clear focus:

> What is it to dwell?
> How does building belong to dwelling?[10]

One can inhabit without dwelling, as one can inhabit an office without making it a home. So what is it that distinguishes these conditions? One of the issues (identified by Adam Sharr[11]) is how architecture is elevated as an art, as a celebrated category, and this is at the root of Heidegger's preference for the more prosaic terms of 'building' and 'dwelling'. When it comes to answering the question 'What is it to dwell?', Heidegger harks back to an almost mythical golden age, when a more 'genuine' form of dwelling (based on his imagination of what one might be like) allowed a connection with the actual construction of a building – an essential connection that has been lost in the modern age.

Experience and perception

While Heidegger falls broadly into the philosophical category of phenomenology, other phenomenological approaches are possible, for example the phenomenology of perception that was pursued by

Maurice Merleau-Ponty. In his definitive work on the subject, *The Phenomenology of Perception*, Merleau-Ponty gives his intention for this phenomenology as being 'a matter of describing, not of explaining or analyzing'.[12]

> Phenomenology is the study of essences; and according to it all problems amount to finding definitions of essences: the essence of perception, or the essence of consciousness, for example. But phenomenology is also a philosophy that puts essences back into existence and does not expect to arrive at an understanding of man and the world from any other starting point other than that of their *facticity*.[13] [my emphasis].

Merleau-Ponty defines *sensation* as the basic unit of perception, this unit being fundamentally different from a stimulus, the external cause of a sensation. We are, in pursuit of the perceptual experience of architecture, dealing with sensations rather than stimuli. The subjective perception, rather than the objective thing that exists in reality for all.

> When the apparent size of an object varies with apparent distance, or its apparent colour with our recollections of the object, it is recognised that the sensory processes are not immune to central influences. In this case, therefore, the 'sensible' cannot be defined as the immediate effect of an external stimulus.[14]

This *sensation* is a useful abstraction, and a purposely convenient one. By examining the sensations experienced in a particular context, at a certain time, and under certain conditions, a more comprehensive account of the experience of that place is given. By surveying architecture and attending to the sensations at various salient positions, or recording the flow of perception along a given route, we can produce an accurate description of how experience unfolds over the course of time.

> The visible is what is seized upon with the eyes, the sensible is what is seized on by the senses.[15]

This active concept of perception is particularly important, describing the processes of perception as being alert rather than passive. This outmoded model of passivity is, according to James Gibson, one of the most substantial errors in the understanding of perception presented by pre-1960s psychology, where controlled laboratory environments are used to assess the senses much as if they were reflexes, automatic reactions to stimuli.[16] Gibson states that our senses are much more complex than this, and he reconsiders the classical model of five senses as *perceptual systems* with a more active character, seeking and searching for sensation rather than passively accommodating them.

> The classical concept of a sense organ is of a passive receiver, and it is called a receptor. But the eyes, ears, nose, mouth, and skin are

in fact mobile, exploratory, orienting. Their input to the nervous system will normally have a component produced by their own activity. The photographic camera is an analogue to a passive receptor. But the eye is not a camera; it is a self-focusing, self-setting, and self-orienting camera whose image becomes optimal because the system compensates for blur, for extremes of illumination, and for being aimed at something uninteresting. This fact might seem to complicate hopelessly an understanding of how the senses work, but the intermixture of externally produced and activity-produced stimulation promises to be the clue to an understanding of how the perceptual systems might work.[17]

Gibson's work has been hugely influential in other fields with regards to his theory of affordances in design, but the perceptual systems are gaining favour with anthropological research into place and environment, such as Tim Ingold's *Perception of the Environment*, which might be more accurately titled *Perception 'in' the Environment*.[18] Ingold notes that there is no perception without context: that the act of perception is inextricable from where it happens, when it happens and under what conditions. A more poetic example can be found in the fiction of Italo Calvino, particularly *Mr. Palomar* and *Under a Jaguar Sun*:

> In short, it would be all very well for you to sing: no one would hear you, they would not hear you, your song, your voice. They would be listening to the king, in the way a king must be listened to, receiving what comes from above and has no meaning beyond the unchanging relationship between him who is above and those who are below. Even she, the sole addressee of your song, could not hear you: yours would not be the voice she hears; she would listen to the king, her body frozen in a curtsey, with the smile prescribed by protocol masking a preconceived rejection.[19]

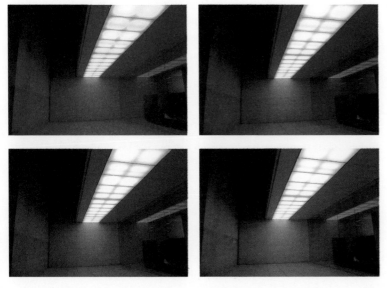

The CaixaForum in Barcelona, with the entrance remodelled by Arata Isozaki. The lighting scheme is constantly changing, giving a different character to the space in a way that moves beyond simplistic ideas of a fixed geometry.

Case study: Sensory notation

Research into the phenomenology of perception and related concepts of sensory perception resulted in the production of a system of notation for architecture and urban design in a project titled 'Multimodal Representation of Urban Space' – a collaboration between the Design, Manufacture & Engineering Management (DMEM) and Architecture departments at the University of Strathclyde. The project was funded jointly by the Arts and Humanities Research Council (AHRC) and the Economic and Social Research Council (ESRC) under the banner of *Designing for the 21st Century*.[20] The project began with the proposition that design practices in architecture and urban design are primarily visual in focus, and that a more holistic approach taking account of all of the senses was more valuable.

A number of approaches were considered before arriving at the design of a notational system, supplemental to conventional architectural drawings. This methodology allowed for research into design practices in a proactive manner. Designing a simple, elegant, but useful and detailed form of representation for sensory perception is a substantial challenge, given the problems encountered when discussing a single sense, such as hearing, in detail.

Working with the team of Professor Wolfgang Sonne (architecture), Gordon Mair (DMEM) and Dr Ombretta Romice (Urban Design), and an advisory board with wide expertise and experience, I investigated urban representation techniques ranging from Giambattista Nolli's plan of Rome, through Kevin Lynch's *Image of the City*, Gordon Cullen's *Townscape*, and beyond to Mario Gandelsonas' morphological studies and Philip Thiel's scores for architecture.[21] Each had its benefits, and a form of Laban movement notation was used for an initial attempt.[22] However, this proved inelegant, too weighty visually, and difficult to learn. This generated further criteria for the eventual notation:

> A simple system, quick to learn, not tied to a particular discipline.
> Something that represents all of the senses at once.
> Notations that work with the existing practices of orthographic drawing.
> An analogy with sketching, requiring no technological mediation.

Other criteria emerged as time went on, but the system had to be simple enough to learn in a brief one-hour workshop, and to work alongside existing practices. The work became avowedly subjective at this stage, and this remains one of the most common questions in workshops: is it possible to produce a sensory notation that is objective, given the nature of the material? This is possible to answer within the context of the present system, as will be shown later, but it sets out its stall as essentially subjective and personal. We cannot know absolutely the details of how another person perceives identical phenomena.

The system was tested with undergraduate and postgraduate students, taken out to geographers and anthropologists, and further developed in terms of its applicability and theoretical implications. The idea of the sketchbook and the pattern book pervade the intention of the research; taking Christopher Alexander's 'Pattern Language' as a model, the aim was to record impressions of places when travelling. Researcher Fei Chen documented several Chinese cities, and I have produced notations of UK cities, including London, Edinburgh, Glasgow and Manchester, as well as some further afield – Tokyo, Seoul, Jakarta, Boston and Rome. Finding viable patterns in these locations has proved interesting in itself, but the system of recording serves the purpose of bedding the experience in the memory firmly, and of opening up that experience to reuse or as a reference point for design.

The notation has three main phases to it, conceptualized as a way of *organizing perception*:

> Document the context, with the date and time, the weather conditions and a plan of the site that shows the locations where notations have been made. These are normally numbered at least 1 to 6, if not more, and can either represent a route taken across a place, or show the variety of conditions around a given place such as a city square or a restaurant. A section is added as best practice, giving valuable volumetric information.

> For each location, use the sensory priority chart: a simple radar chart that measures the priority that the researcher places on each sense from 1 to 6. The senses are reorganized to be more relevant to architecture: Visual, Aural, Tactile, Kinetic, Thermal and Chemical. Additional marks can be made to indicate certain temporal qualities to the chart, and a list of non-metaphorical terminology is also provided to give further quick description of each location.

> It is essential to write and photograph the site in addition to the above. The graphic means are essentially reductive and give no value judgements regarding the space in question. It is more efficient to simply write about the place – somewhere in the region of 1,500 words of flat, straightforward description.

There is more detail, contained within the guide to the notation.[23] The question of the later uses of the notations is interesting, and the subjectivity question can be overcome when the sensory survey is used within a group context. By having several notators conduct a sensory survey together, they can be asked to produce individual results and combine them later, or to use it as the basis of an *in situ* discussion. Each of these has its benefits, as does the individualistic investigation of a site through diagrams and writing. A number of interesting ideas have been investigated using this method, such as a paper investigating the differences between two different sacred spaces in Tokyo, which have

some broad geometric and functional similarities, but radically different
characters in reality, which can be clearly expressed in sensory terms.

The design of the system raised a number of questions about our
visual bias, the geometric bias and the way in which we ignore certain
elements of the built environment. The aim was to heighten awareness
of this and to develop a means of investigation rather than to radically
overhaul the professional practice of architecture. The system remains
in development with this aim in mind, and potential automation of
elements using crowd-sourced mobile applications as a supplement to
the manual systems described above.

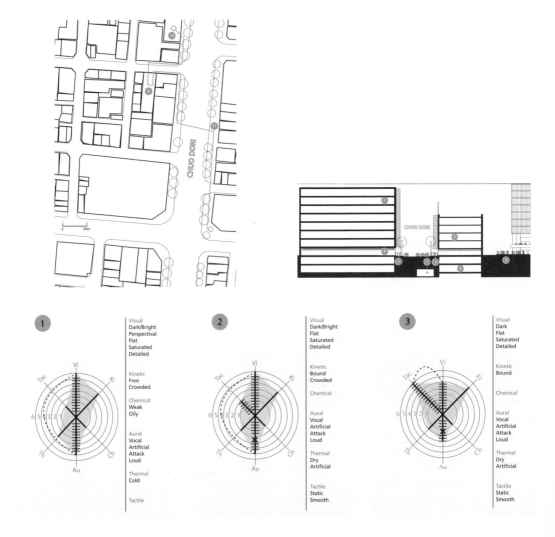

Accompanying photographs
of Akihabara, from sensory
notation of Tokyo.

Chapter 13:
Ethnographic research

Ethnography is a longitudinal and subjective study, where the researcher spends extended periods in the field, interacting and recording in various ways in order to find out more about a given context. A methodology closely associated with anthropology, ethnography is somewhat discipline-agnostic, and can be used by a wide range of academic fields.

Ethnography is largely untapped as a form of research in architecture, but it has a great deal of potential in urban design and post-occupancy studies, and there are many further uses for this methodology in architecture and the built environment.

Translating the findings of such research is challenging, particularly as ethnography depends on an open-minded researcher, who is there to observe and interact, but not to pass judgement or to say what is right or wrong. This chapter presents some ways of reading ethnographic studies, and how to use the literature generated. Important work is readily available in urban anthropology, the anthropology of the home and other specifically sited works, offering insights into the different ways of being human that co-exist in the world.

This chapter also presents research into the anthropology of creative practice, working auto-ethnographically in the design studio environment, anthropological seminar and at the drawing board.

Conducting ethnographic research

Ethnographic research is an empirical method closely associated with fieldwork, and should be approached with the material covered in Chapter 5 in mind.[1] That said, it is a very specific and longitudinal study of a particular context that needs careful planning and consideration as well as an openness to serendipity and happenstance.

Ethnography allows the researcher access to other people's lives – how they practise them and engage with their context. With any social research, the problem of precisely how to get people to say this can be rather more difficult, as people often play down the aspects of their lives that they are uncomfortable with, or that they simply feel are so self-evident as to be uninteresting to anyone else. The aim of the ethnographic methodology is to cut through the differences between what people say and what they actually do. In most cases there will be quite a gap between these two things, and for a variety of reasons. Both the deliberate presentation, the reality of what happens, and the reasons for this disjunction are interesting research issues, and should be addressed. One of the keys to this is the time that ethnography takes, typically lasting from months to years; the contemporary model of ethnography involves living with people and sharing their lifestyle while taking part and observing simultaneously.

What people say they do, in interviews. This reflects the way that people wish to be seen. This can lead, for example, to a refusal to admit to poverty, or the presentation of as positive a message as possible, as a matter of pride or social status.

What people actually do in everyday life. This can be witnessed through direct empirical observation. Access may be difficult, due to informants knowing that there is a mismatch between their verbal account and reality. At other times, access may be restricted due to illegality or expertise: it would be dangerous to have someone unskilled in a factory environment or trawler, for example.

The reasons why these differ, through theory and analysis. Part of the task of ethnography is to move beyond description and reportage and towards consideration of some of the reasons why certain things are the case. Misrepresentations should not be taken for lies or in any other pejorative sense, but rather as fascinating insights into how people choose to represent themselves to others.

Ethnography is about people, first and foremost, so any reference to context is always related to what it can tell you about the people who live there, or their interactions with that environment. In this kind of research, the people you encounter are normally referred to as *informants*. The arrival in an unfamiliar site is fraught with uncertainty, and ethnographic researchers must rely on a variety of methods to identify potential informants – some ahead of time, others once you arrive. Not every relationship between researcher and informant will be fruitful, so it is important to cast your net relatively wide.

Strategies for identifying initial informants will vary according to your research, but it is unusual for a researcher to have an interest in a context without having some established connection to the place, so this is a natural place to start: with the people you already know. Speculative letters to academics and local groups and associations can also provide some initial contacts, as can posting advertisements in local shop windows, in newspapers or on online message boards. Each informant can lead to further contacts, and a network of people usually makes itself apparent.

It is essential to be clear with any potential informant of your role as a researcher, putting their mind to rest about your intentions. There can be many reasons why anyone would be uneasy with such attention – unregulated market activities that could be exposed problematically, or interpersonal relationships that are strained between one person and another, for example – so you should be prepared to offer your informants the opportunity to read work ahead of publication, or to be anonymized in the accounts given. The people you are working with need to be able to trust your motives.

Key processes can be identifying formal and informal *gatekeepers* to sites and informants. These can be research institutions that review and control access to vulnerable informants, or respected leaders of any community who carry enough weight to give you tacit permission to speak to others within a group.

Once access has been gained, there are several ways to proceed. Some ethnography relies upon structured or free-flowing interviews, meeting informants and asking them directly about certain aspects of their everyday life. This is often more of a preamble than a full ethnography, which is increasingly associated with participant observation, where you will essentially apprentice yourself to an informant, working alongside them, learning how certain parts of life are managed here and what skills are required to go along with this life-world.

Writing Culture

An important set of papers on anthropological methodology, published as *Writing Culture*,[2] provide a wealth of insights. Edited by James Clifford and George Marcus, these papers delineate a theory of anthropology as an attempt to *write* culture. This initially simple notion becomes more complex once one begins to unpack the full meaning. The product of the anthropological project is a piece of writing (sometimes other things, too, such as films and photographs, largely on the grounds opened up by this debate). That anthropologists produce writing was never really challenged until the seminar series and subsequent essay collection (first published in 1986), and the ongoing debates that this provoked.[3]

An interesting aside is to consider what constitutes an academic debate. Often a position will be developed within a department that is different to the established norm. In order to fully develop this, conferences with like-minded academics are organized, and more intimate seminars or series of invited lectures are used to consolidate and discuss the detail of an idea before presenting it in a series of books or edited collections of papers, generally representing a particular event or series. Such publications and journal articles are subject to review by the broader community, inevitably leading to support, adaptation or outright opposition of the ideas presented. Thus, the debate becomes polarized through publication of articles, reviews, and even letters. This occurs within any academic discipline, including architecture.

In *Writing Culture*, Clifford and Marcus examine the quality of writing used by anthropologists. Quality, here, does not just concern the merits of the writing, but the very character of that writing. The contention is that the writing of anthropologists ought to convey the experience of fieldwork more fully. Rather than attempting to neutralize the feelings of the anthropologist, the authors recognize that there is something essential in conveying the purely subjective nature of the encounter. This is in opposition to the scientific model of writing, and more akin to biography or even fiction writing. The academy took some time to become accustomed to this notion, that such accounts could be poetic and yet rigorous examinations of culture at the same time. Anthropology is, by nature, an extremely personal and subjective experience. However much the researcher would like to be objective (and this is in itself a questionable desire, as already discussed with reference to fieldwork and ethnography), there is always a trace of their personality in the account. The choices made, the places and situations the researcher ends up in, are all entirely contextualized by the researcher's agency.

It is important to underline that context denotes the set of circumstances that you find yourself in. This includes the self – all your own prejudices and attitudes – as well as the specific site, the time and weather, the position in your own histories. Context is too often (but not always) erased from modernist approaches to design and research, but it has become apparent that this is a huge mistake, for context is what allows anything to make any sense at all.

One of the things *Writing Culture* was concerned with was the notion of ethnographic authority, whereby an absolute account of a culture was suggested by the style of writing. This power of depiction to control the depicted is deeply problematic, particularly with the deepening critique of colonial power relations within the discipline. Put simply, the way that you choose to represent things is important, and it is possible to present a falsely complete picture, or to sound authoritative on a topic that has as many points of view as there are practitioners. Anthropology, unlike philosophy, which it is closely related to, confirms that there is no singular truth, but many simultaneous ways of being – the very term of truthfulness being somewhat misleading.

Using ethnographic research by others

Ethnographic research is available to researchers as a resource and, while it often speaks to the discipline of anthropology most directly, there are things that researchers in architecture can glean from such enquiries. The reasons for doing so are pragmatic: it is an area of expertise that is tied to social science disciplines, and while the focus of such research might not always suit the needs of architectural research, the detail and longitudinal nature of such investigations is extremely valuable.

The ethnographic account is authoritative, within the bounds of its investigation. This is to say that generalization of the results of an ethnographic research project can be a little fraught, as the cultural specificity is often part of the point of the research, but when researching urban marketplaces, for example, the accounts produced by Theodore Bestor [4], Rachel Black [5] and Michèle de la Pradelle [6] are all instructive in both theory and pertinent ethnographic detail. The key is not to make too large a claim for any similarities you find between the context you are interested in, and the one that you are reading about. Comparisons might be possible, and correlations useful, but remain cautious.

Other accounts can be instructive when considering design practices. In considering the home, Inge Daniels[7] and Sarah Pink[8] have both taken different approaches to the ethnography of dwelling.

Pink's work takes the idea of the gender of space, and explores how conventional ideas of this need to be updated and included in a more generalized model of home-making activity as an active production of identity. Understanding the European home (with examples mainly from the UK and Spain) as a set of practices and processes is derived directly from the ethnographic evidence, and this assists Pink in understanding the ways in which identity is also a process, a flow or movement rather than a stable core.

By contrast, Daniels discusses the flow of materials through the home. Taking the culturally specific circumstances of Japanese homes (largely in Osaka), Daniels notes the way in which culturally significant practices of gift-giving are accommodated within the Japanese home. Storage becomes enormously important, and innovative solutions include small cupboards inserted into the ceilings to save on precious floorspace. Other issues are raised in this examination, such as the accommodation of both traditional *tatami*-style rooms and Western-influenced bedrooms, which challenge the fundamentals of family life in interesting ways, but which were initially the result of a deliberate policy intent on modernizing the Japanese family by bringing it into line with Western norms.

The ethnographies of other researchers are important resources, too, and should be consulted both for the finer details of their daily accounts and the theorizations that follow. This can inform your own research greatly, but take care not to extrapolate too far, as the stated aim of ethnographic research is to investigate the cultural specificity of a given context.

Case study: Ethnographies of creative practice – experiment or ethnography?

Some research questions require alternative approaches, one of which is deemed a form of auto-ethnography (à la autobiography, see Deborah Reed-Danahay[9], and Anne Meneley and Donna Young[10]), although others prefer to consider it a kind of experimental method. Whatever the nomenclature, such research methods are useful for interrogating issues such as creative practice, questioning the ways in *which* different kinds of drawing and diagramming allow for innovation and improvisation. With this in mind, I often work in this experimental/auto-ethnographic mode. Grouping forms of drawing and graphic work together as *inscriptive practices*, I have produced a number of examples of this, which are detailed below.

These inscriptive practice projects were designed alongside a written text, representing a continuous dialogue between the textual and the graphic. Given that one central premise of these projects is that inscriptive practices can be used just as well as writing, to develop theory, it was wholly appropriate, and indeed necessary, to engage in such practices. This was particularly so, given my background in architecture, meaning drawings, diagrams and notations are a large part of my practice. The mutual interplay held between graphic and written inscriptions allowed the argument of this thesis to develop. The inscription projects are not intended simply as proofs or demonstrations of the written theories; rather, they were instrumental in developing the theoretical standpoint of the text. An extended negotiation between the forms of thinking represented by text and graphic inscription informs the entire thesis.

The first project grew out of a prior interest in film and architecture (Lucas[11]), beginning with a series of sketchbooks, each looking at a particular film, and examining it on similar terms. The sketchbooks were completed rapidly, as I set myself the task of drawing synchronously to the film. The sketches were made in graphite, a particularly quick and expressive medium that does not allow for fiddly details to emerge, leaving only broad, gestural marks.

Out of these sketchbooks, a scene from Kurosawa's *Seven Samurai* emerged as particularly interesting, and I chose to pursue this further by completing a Laban[12] movement notation of the scene. This allowed for subsequent translations beyond the original intention of simply learning Laban notation by using it. It also allowed for creative adaptation,

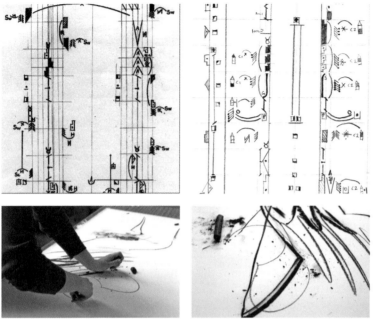

Seven Samurai notation and drawing, and the Hospitalfield House performance and drawing workshop with artist Sandra McNeil.

leading me to translate the movements of the actors from the film scene into a series of hand movements that would be appropriate for an artist colleague to make with charcoal on paper. These marks were given as verbal instructions at the Creativity and Practice Group's Hospitalfield House workshop event in January 2003.[13] The separation of the observation, instruction and autographic mark in this project allowed for sustained reflection on the nature of notation.

The next project was much more modest, and continued my attempts to learn more about Laban notation. The task in this case was to notate a Sumo bout observed on a trip to Tokyo. Laban notation was used to describe the actions of several participants in each highly ritualized bout – the announcer, the judge and the two fighters. Notating the bout was achieved by observing photographs, video footage and memories of my time watching the wrestlers. Once again, the practice of observation was implicated strongly and channelled by Laban notation, directing my attention from the most generalized postural aspects of the movement through to subtle movements such as the referee's fan. The process of fighting a bout of Sumo rather than any particular match was to be notated, showing that Laban is capable of generalizations and conditional movement as well as strictly prescribed sets of actions. The inclusion of triggering events, such as those used to begin the fight, proved rather important in my understanding of Laban for subsequent projects, and showed the creative potential of Laban to record complex and uncertain events.

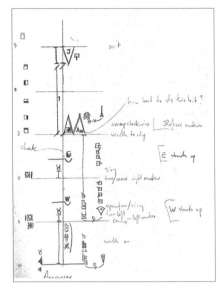
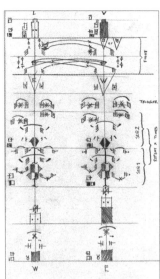
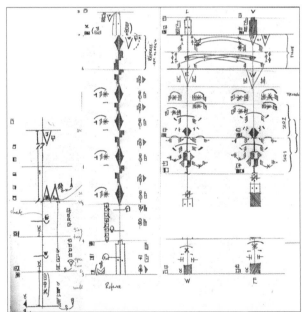
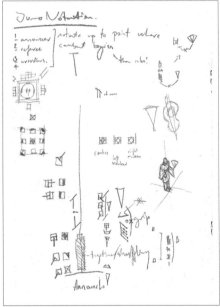

Sumo notation, showing the initial sketches and simplified scores through to final notation.

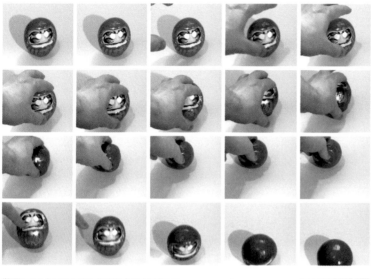

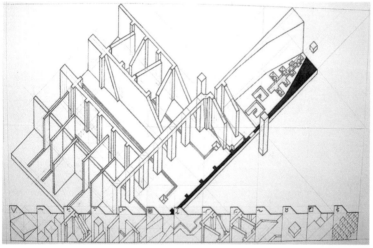

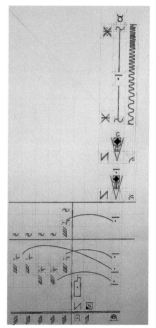

Another project was undertaken for the group exhibition 'Fieldnotes and Sketchbooks', held at Aberdeen Art Gallery from April to June 2005, and is presented in more detail in the collected volume edited by curator and researcher Wendy Gunn.[14] This project focused on a *Daruma* doll from Japan. The *Daruma* doll is explained in greater detail elsewhere, but I found several movements involving the artefact to be of particular interest: the mixing of ink; painting of an eye; and rocking backwards and forwards. I noted these actions, again using Laban notation. I also made short videos and arranged frame captures from this footage in sequence. These images were assembled into both a storyboard and flick-books. The Laban notation allowed a translation process to be undertaken, eventually making an architectural space from my observations of the rocking movement. The final process of description was a much more immediate ink drawing, simply making a gestural mark on paper in response to the movement in real time.

Gestural Artefacts: Notations of a Daruma Doll. Notations, axonometric drawing and calligraphic drawing, all describing the movement shown by the video frame captures.

This collection of descriptions allowed a direct comparison to be made between inscriptive practices, and allowed particularly detailed reflections on the temporality of automated recordings such as video by comparison with observationally based drawing or notation. The role of the spectator was also considered in more detail, as the level of engagement could be understood in terms of one's ability to reconstruct the process of making a particular mark. In this regard, the ink drawing had the greatest impact, and the Laban, which required greater specialized knowledge to understand, made less of an impression.

Each of these projects was more about an understanding of my own creative practice than about the observed phenomenon: not about the Kurosawa film, the junior Sumo bout or the *Daruma* doll, but about how I responded to these graphically. These investigations reveal something of the spatial character of each event, discussed according to bodies in motion rather than engineered structures. The role of the inscriptive practices, multiple in each case, was documented in a step-by-step fashion, reflecting upon each step of the process and eventually discussing the crucial role of temporality in creative practice. This theorization would not have been possible without the process of documentation and field notes that accompanied each inscription project, so the ethnographic practice – even if not a full ethnography – is what opened up each practice and made it available for consideration and theorization.

銀座線渋谷駅事務室
地下鉄お忘れ物取扱所
Subway Lost & Found

Chapter 14: Drawing, diagrams and maps

As media native to architecture, what do inscriptive practices such as drawing have to offer as research methods? As a preamble to fully practice-based research, what does it mean to appreciate the graphic work as being both appropriate and capable of producing knowledge in architecture?

There are a great many examples of this, but research all too often remains wholly in the domain of the written word. This chapter presents some of the problems and benefits of working with drawings, diagrams, maps and notations in your research: how to present such work, allowing it to enter into dialogue with a text. Practical issues such as the legibility of a diagram and the competence of readers to approach it shall be addressed, and some insights into research by way of drawing.

This book supports the idea that there can be an architectural research that uses the tools of architectural production as a means for describing, theorizing and explaining. This chapter makes explicit the possibilities for drawing, diagramming, notation, cartography and other graphic representations in the research process, bringing the results of research closer to the design process.

More than merely supporting illustrations, drawings such as these can be understood as research, and as architectural theory. To this end, my project, 'Getting Lost in Tokyo', an exhibition consisting of diagrams, notations, drawings and paintings, will be discussed alongside other examples.

A practice native to architecture

Drawing is one of the practices native to architecture, and is one that is well placed towards research as a method of investigation, as a form of dissemination, and also as the focus for study. There is a long tradition of the *paper project* in architecture, and this forms the foundation of research by drawing. Setting a proposition down on paper in the form of a design is one way to confront the challenges of a set of circumstances or a peculiar context, and the paper project offers the researcher the freedom to consider extreme examples such as the *War and Architecture* drawings of Lebbeus Woods, *Manhattan Transcripts* of Bernard Tschumi, *Micromegas* by Daniel Libeskind, or various series by John Hejduk, including *Adjusting Foundations* and *Victims*.[1]

Most notable among architects who research by drawing would be Peter Eisenman. Establishing his project as an architect is his PhD thesis, *The Formal Basis of Modern Architecture,* and further explorations through

Page 174: The subway sign that inspired 'Getting Lost in Tokyo' (see page 178).

Below: A sample of some of my drawings from a variety of projects, showing a diversity of approaches.

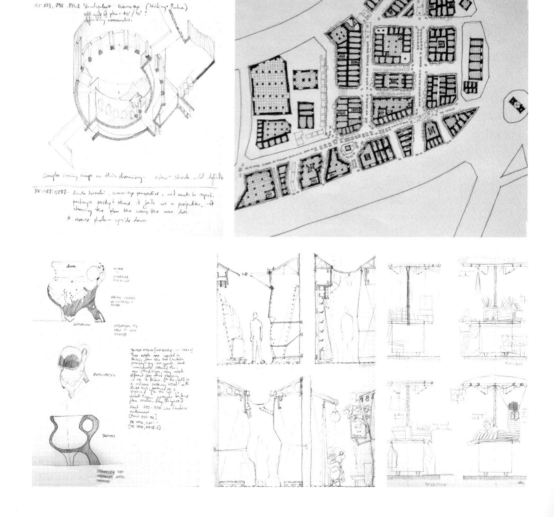

drawing and diagram in *Ten Canonical Buildings*.[2] Eisenman's early houses worked between drawing and models in a way that was exploratory and experimental, asking the same questions he found in the deconstructionist theory of Deleuze, but in a distinctively architectonic fashion.

Architectural research can be conducted and communicated by means other than the written text. While the meaning of a text can be rendered straightforward and enables a directness of communication, there are a great many benefits to the graphic representation native to architecture as a discipline.

To this end, it is useful to discuss an example that asked deliberate questions of representation and translation from one form of drawing to another, translations from the intentions of the draughtsman to the viewer.

The sketchbook as a storeroom for ideas

> Look in the notebooks of any great architect and you will see a 'magpie' acquiring ideas from wherever they may be found, playing with them and taking possession of them.[3]

Simon Unwin is an architect and writer who makes extensive use of his own sketchbooks in exploring architectural issues and theory. Unwin describes his notebook as 'a storeroom for ideas'[4] and as a

> laboratory for investigating and appreciating, through drawing, the qualitative aspects of experiencing places and their ambience: light and shade; reflection; texture; mood...[5]

His use of drawing to depict elements of fundamental architectural interest is often misread by his peers as a simplistic introductory approach to architecture, but his work is, in fact, by virtue of this approach, valuable to the novice and expert alike. The difference in understanding can often be said to lie in the quality with which one is able to read the drawings.

Unwin discusses the nature of the sketchbook itself in the collection *Fieldnotes and Sketchbooks*, edited by Wendy Gunn. It is here that he develops the idea of the search in sketching.

> The mind of a Searcher is moulded by its Searches. Drawn to explore by an inkling that there is something to discover, its evolving understanding is modified by encounters with what it finds.[6]

To Unwin, the sketchbook has each of these different facets, as varied and pregnant with possibilities. Each of these descriptions speaks to the different ways in which the notebook contains and carries our thoughts:

as something to be seen as sacred, but profane at the same time. A solemn experience or one full of pleasure. Is it a puzzle, an enigma or a joke? Is it the ground for exercise or relaxation?

The answer to Unwin is all of these things and probably several more. He approaches the notebook as a research tool, one that approaches fundamental and basic elements of architecture such as composition, thresholds, massing, form, experience. With the sketchbook, he seeks these elements out and then explores them through the experience of recording them. This is framed by Unwin in the short essay that contains several spreads from his notebook: this enquiry through drawing is a search for knowledge and for meaning.

Over the years, Unwin has compiled a large number of these roughly identical Moleskine notebooks. They are uniform and unassuming, but within each of these are his thoughts and travels. Importantly, he draws and sketches not only in perspective, but also in plan, section and a wide variety of other forms of drawing – all on the one page. Moving between drawing conventions and projections in order to probe and further understand is as important as being able to move efficiently between scales when describing, allowing for the volume, form, texture, relationships, contexts and more to be depicted and understood further through comparison.

This forms a research practice and methodology for Unwin, whose sketchbooks contain the seeds of various overlapping research projects. Indeed the work contained can have multiple meanings and various uses, rather than being effective in a single context only. Unwin's drawings do not have a singular meaning, but represent multiple possibilities.

Case study: 'Getting Lost in Tokyo'

The 'Getting Lost in Tokyo' project concerned the Tokyo subway system and the experience of lostness. A number of issues were addressed by the project, which found its origins in a series of journeys around the system, and was focused on the nodes of Shinjuku and Shibuya stations in particular. Shinjuku is a major node of Tokyo's transportation network, having numerous exits to the surface – vast underground passageways connecting to commercial and business concerns in the area.

The subway sign that started it all: Lost & Found.

In investigating the idea that drawings can be valid forms of research, I worked on the project as an exploration of various theories regarding narrative, embodiment, wayfinding and temporality. The work was exhibited at the Visual Research Centre in Dundee in 2005, and explored in papers published in journals and an edited collection.[7] Like many projects, the initial research question was straightforward: is it possible to represent the space of the intricate and complex Tokyo subway network in a meaningful way?

The challenge of a *meaningful* representation is important to note, as clearly there are representations of the overall network that conform to the standards set down by Harry Beck in 1931 for the London Underground, and elaborated by others over time and across the world. Other representations will conform to the needs of civil and transportation engineers or the operational needs of the system itself, but few representations consider the actual experience of negotiating the subway. Conventional architectural representations do not tell us what we need to know about this, and with this in mind I set about a project to investigate this qualitative aspect of my own experience as an architectural tourist with limited language skills.

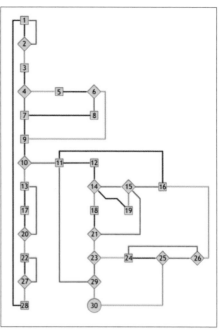

The flowchart, with episodes 1 to 30 described in terms of their relation to one another as a process.

The first move was to construct a process diagram or flowchart of the key events in my experience. This was a necessary abstraction, but one that responded to a clear narrative of the experience. It was clear early on that my interest was not in using the subway once, as a singular experience, but as a set of experiences: an accumulation of using the subway across several journeys. This opens up one front theoretically: the nature of the relationship between *place* and *experience*. In this case, it was most consistent to think of multiples – plural uses of the system – rather than seeing it as a singular event. Much as one might think of cyclical temporality in daily, weekly or seasonal cycles, the subway can only be understood over the course of multiple uses.

One of the benefits of diagramming and drawing is the possibility of translating them into another format, another convention. Each inscriptive practice (a term used in this research to denote not only drawings, but other kinds of graphic work such as notations, diagrams and maps) can be translated into another – in this case from diagram into notation.

The episodic nature of the diagram suggests a structure that subdivides an experience, allows for options and decisions. Each of the discrete events can be depicted on its own terms: Laban movement notation in this case. This form of notation has several notable qualities, and was developed by the choreographer and movement theorist Rudolf von Laban to depict a wide variety of forms of movement, not just traditional ballet.[8] All dance notations are contentious (as they are considered to influence the content or character of the dance depicted), but Laban allows the notator to depict movement from the point of view of the person who is moving at the time, not from the perspective of the audience, as is most common. It is a dense symbolic language, though, and difficult to read without a great deal of research into the system. This renders it rather opaque to most viewers, who can observe that it encodes without knowing precisely what is represented.

This opacity of the notation is not a problem, but merely a quality of it. It is important to understand that this is often a pay-off for precision of information such as that contained within Laban notation; in order to depict the possibility for movement of the human body, a complex system is unavoidable.

In simple terms, the structure of Laban operates as a stave, most often read vertically from the bottom of the page upwards. One stave is given for each individual or group moving together. The left and right sides then read as the corresponding sides of the body, with positions and transitions depicted in order of those required for stability near the centre-line, and increasingly gestural movements described further out from the stave. Laban offers flexibility to the performer, who can have some improvisation and interpretation built into the score.

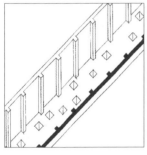
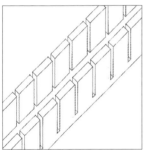

Archetypal Laban notations.

While it might seem odd to be discussing dance notation in a book about architectural research, it is important to recognize the usefulness of different inscriptive practices to your own work. Borrowing styles of drawing or modes of diagramming from other disciplines can be fruitful, particularly when the concerns are so in tune with one another. Architects must, after all, be concerned with how people move in their buildings. Indeed, these concerns are taken on by many architectural theorists who expand the field by inventing notational systems with reference to those found elsewhere, be that mathematical calculations in parametric architecture, the harmony of Classical architecture, which has so much in common with musical notation, or the use of storyboards from cinema in the work of Superstudio and others.[9]

In this case, the Laban notation is a record of my experience: what it felt like to move through each of the episodes described by the initial flowchart. In producing the notations, certain common elements come to the fore – notably, 15 repeated elements. Producing drawings and notations allows some time to digest and consider a process with care and attention; you are able to understand what you have produced more fully. In this case, these 15 elements represent repeated movements, classifications of how I engaged with the environment.

This process of classification or taxonomy allowed the next translation to take place, whereby the 15 elements could be redrawn as architectural elements, axonometric building blocks that could then be recomposed into corridors representing my experience of using the subway.

Translating back into conventional architectural language allows the experience to be understood on those terms, the conditions of movement explored through a variety of gradients, voids, obstacles and doors. This leads to two alternative compositional models, one resembling orchestration, where a variety of inscriptive practices are displayed together in order to holistically depict a single episode. This

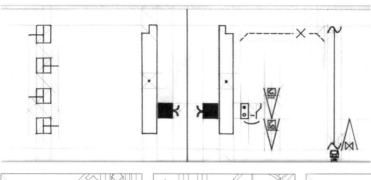

Laban notation episode samples.

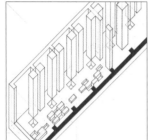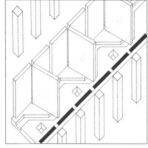

was the main approach of the project: to show the episodic nature of the experience with extracts from the flowchart shown alongside the Laban notation, the axonometric drawing, and with the addition of a photograph that has a similar atmosphere, but in an oblique, associative way.

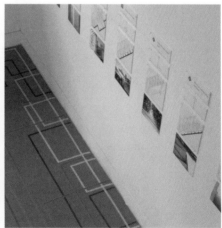

Photograph from the 'Getting Lost in Tokyo' exhibition, showing the series.

Inscriptive practices as qualities rather than categories

Diagrams: Diagrams are often used to describe organizational principles, and can be designed for one-off use or according to a common schema such as flow diagrams. Diagrams show principles and relationships between phenomena, with an underlying structure reflecting the order imposed. Most diagrams can be approached fresh, with the aid of a key to understanding the terms.

Notations: A more explicitly communicative medium, notations consist of a set of instructions that can be performed or repeated, such as a score for music, which can be played. Both the act of composing the script and its performance can be understood as creative acts, commonly conflated with other modes of graphic representation. A degree of expertise is often required to understand a notation, making for a less accessible form of expression than a diagram, but one that is potentially more accurate.

Sketches: Preparatory works that fall into two broad categories. First, sketches can present an immediate response to a context, such as simply sitting and drawing a scene. Second, a sketch might indicate a drawing made in order to develop an idea, often to a self-referential schema not accessible or intended for others to read clearly.

Drawings: Drawings are a broad category, which denotes a certain pictorial quality and often simply describes 'works on paper'. Such an everyday term can be considered contentious and open to definition, but it is worth remembering that – as with all inscriptive practices – the production of a drawing can have a cognitive role, allowing the practitioner to think in graphic terms. Drawing conventions are particularly important in architecture, each with different demands and affordances.

Maps, plans and cartography: The spatialization of data is denoted by mapping. This can be understood in a variety of ways, of course, but the notion of a territory is measured and delineated by a map, giving a sense of scale as well as describing a border condition of inclusion and exclusion.

Pictures: Pictures are, like the above, qualities rather than categories of inscriptive practice, and can be said to denote the mimesis or resemblance a depiction has to something in the world. This can operate to validate the possibility of a work of architecture, to make it feel more real.

Images: Subject to a great many theories, images are often discussed as fleeting and objectifying qualities of the visual field. Other theories consider images as a superior form of representation, where a temporal aspect is included or a deeper logic demonstrated fully. Anthropologist Alfred Gell discussed the notion that a trap for an animal is a perfect image of it; and philosopher Gilles Deleuze describes a clock as an image as it keeps up with time, as opposed to a photograph of a clock, which is a depiction of one point in time. [10]

Drawing research methods

Copying: Copying is an age-old method for understanding a drawing, and one that – in this age of mechanical or digital reproduction (with a nod to the famous Walter Benjamin essay) – is often overlooked, but retracing a well-known drawing is an excellent way to interrogate it, approaching drawing on its own terms and examining qualities of composition, proportion, line quality and shade.

Collaborating: Collaborative drawing is helpful in allowing a dialogue to emerge between participants. This can take the form of drawings based upon a classic exemplar, discussing a commonly understood work, but with the verbal content supplanted by a graphic or visual understanding.

Drawing attention: Using drawing as a way to understand a phenomenon more directly is also valuable. This relies upon an understanding of the drawing as a way of meditating on a scene or event – a focused attention that allows overlooked details to emerge. The simple act of drawing an object in an orthographic projection tells you about the form and materiality of an object, supplementing any historical or material culture research you might do.

Drawing is not only an appropriate form of investigation, but one that allows for entirely different forms of knowledge to emerge. Sometimes this can be through continual practices of drawing in order to find out and understand, while at other times the intention will be to intervene or propose something through the medium of drawing. Drawing encompasses such a wide range of practices that your methodological statement might usefully explore the qualities of the drawing you are engaged in: the notational or pictorial aspects, autographic qualities or aleatory processes. Each of these qualities communicates something, and allows you to make informed choices not only about *what* you draw, but also *how you do it*.

The Labyrinth, which depicts the complete series, showing how useful the episodes are in managing the context.

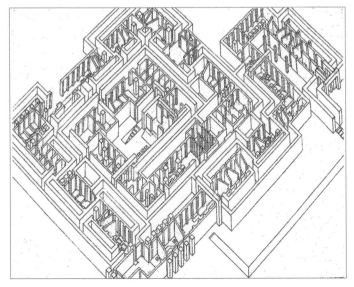

Chapter 15: Conclusion: Theory and practice

Professional architectural practice has different pressures from academia, but the need for research is still keenly felt. Much of the research is produced in practice, with practitioners being best placed to conduct grounded, practical investigations into architecture.

The investigation of a context – socially, physically or historically – remains a part of the architectural discipline, as one must know about a place in order to make a sensible intervention there. Assessing and meeting the needs of clients and users, understanding a building for reuse, or working with precedents in order to produce more engaging architectural spaces are all founded on good research.

The connection between academic research and architectural practice is becoming more common and formalized, with growing numbers of opportunities for practice-based PhD research, and Knowledge Transfer Partnerships (KTP) schemes offering opportunities to reduce the distance and time between research and practice.

While the focus of this book has been on the student experience of research, it is essential to draw a connection with architectural practice, demonstrating how such work is utilized outside the academic context. The relationship between commercial architectural practice and research is an interesting one, and a wide range of collaborations are possible. It is therefore important to conclude with a forward-looking account of how architects conduct research, how it is used and why it is important.

Two architects, Robert Adam and Craig Dykers, have been interviewed formally in this regard – questioned about the approach taken to architecture and how it informs their work. Robert Adam is a leading urban designer and architect who maintains a close relationship with several UK universities, taking a strong interest in the development of both disciplines.[1] What is particularly interesting about Adam is that he actively pursues research both as an individual, and also as part of a body that can commission research on a variety of issues. Recent work has included a piece describing trends in urban design. This research established a methodology that allows one to understand the underlying masterplanning as part of a social movement rather than individual expressions.

Social trends and their development are also important to Adam's work as a designer. He sees the lifetime of a building in the round rather than at the singular point of its execution. Hiring a sociologist to work within his practice resulted in a report that begins to understand family composition and home ownership in the post-credit crunch era.

Adam is interested in the utility of this research, and, being a professional architect, he must respond not only to these lines of enquiry, but he must also consider what value is added to his design practice as a result: there is always a bottom line to his investigations, a practicality lying behind the research.

> **RA:** In the end, a rather interesting aspect of academia – of which I am greatly fond – is that, actually, practice and academia have a rather curious relationship: basically, I have to make money, in simple terms. So I have to bring stuff forward on the basis either that I'm spending money in a quasi-charitable fashion, which is quite difficult to say that I am doing; or that I am actually advancing something which will have a financial value.
>
> As you get bigger – and quite a few firms do this – as you get bigger, of course, the definition of financial value begins to shift. A *reputation* has a financial value, but it is slightly intangible. So, for example, this social research we are producing – what value will it have for us?
>
> The first one was the masterplanning study – what value does this have? We have come up with a methodology which we hope to encourage students to use in order to develop it. What it has done, is that it's improved our standing in the urban design community, the wider urban design community. That's quite intangible.
>
> You will never ever prove that it is making you money. But if you are big enough, you can absorb it: people's perception of you changes. The same goes for the social research, which will be directed towards housing. We will be able to go to people in housing and say 'you must realise that we understand the way in which this market is moving'. And so that has a benefit. It might never ever win us a job, so this is going to cost us £——— I suppose, but you know ...

Research partnerships are also a significant aspect of Adam's practice. Working with the University of Strathclyde, and addressing a perceived issue with the development of Space Syntax tools, Adam understood that the computational analysis was based on some rather outdated assumptions, and that an opportunity for some newer tools was available.[2]

> **RA:** For example, we paid £—— I think. We were very precise about it, bringing forward a piece of research which we got from the University of Strathclyde and the University of Lausanne, which we called Place Logic, which is a digital systems analysis of urban flows, of movement flows. There's a thing called Space Syntax, which is the same thing but it is using an out-of-date systems analysis, about a 30-year-old systems analysis.

Craig Dykers is a partner in the global architecture firm Snøhetta, and has a substantially different relationship with research.[3] Notably, Snøhetta has been the subject of research more than once: anthropologists have worked within this practice in order to investigate the nature of creativity within the studio environment, conducting longitudinal studies such as ethnographies and participant observation. Dykers' understanding of the value of this process is particularly interesting: he sees such studies as a kind of therapy or reflective process for the practice itself, and believes that by questioning and understanding the social process of architectural design they can adapt as a practice and continue to develop their approach. Dykers has a personal form of research practice in addition to this, one that he is somewhat self-deprecating about, but which will be familiar to many architects: he has an enquiring mind and an appetite for broad-based knowledge about the world. This is not instrumental, and does not need to have a direct relationship to his design practice; there is a degree of faith that its relevance will emerge in a more holistic manner.

> **CD:** In terms of the aim and what is valuable for us, it is more in the sense of nudging things along. I know that we have had a few anthropologists along in our office, after Wendy [Gunn] was here. I would say in the history of our office, we have probably had five or six, maybe seven, anthropologists sitting in our office from time to time. One of the most extensive studies was based on four months in Norway and three months in New York – and we got the reports back, they were very interesting. When I read through them, we discovered things about ourselves – it was more like a psychiatrist...
>
> **RL:** Like therapy for your practice?
>
> **CD:** They nudged us in different ways and different directions, different ways of thinking.
>
> **RL:** So did that have a tangible effect on how the office operated?
>
> **CD:** Oh yes, definitely. Just thinking of one example: there was a

discussion about laughter, and when laughter occurred and when it didn't, and how laughter was used in context, which isn't necessarily directed at us. I think everyone at some point in their work day has times when they may laugh or not. In our office, it may be a little different to other architecture offices; there tend to be slightly more jovial conditions. They were talking about what that means and what it means to the working process as a social process.

We found out that having that as a part of our routine was allowing for a kind of openness, to let people feel they are comfortable enough to have some humour in the creative endeavours which we undertake.

RL: Do you think that anthropologists taking part in the studio in different ways – has that made you quite reflective as a practitioner?

CD: Absolutely.

RL: So that you are very much interested in the design process.

CD: Oh yes, I think it's great. Strangely enough, anthropology has been losing ground over the last decade and some universities have even been taking it off the curriculum, which I really don't understand.

RL: It's been a tough time for the discipline. Does the practice actually commission research? Do you just wait and see who wants to work with you?

CD: Yes and no – again, I am really sheepish about saying that our office has any kind of research thread. There are offices which are much more rigorous. I think we are deliberate in the way in which we approach development and research. We tend to thread it through our daily life rather than segregate it. It tends to be more informal and I think we like it that way. We're the kind of company that – it's kind of our root, our core belief system is that we want to create architecture that gets built within highly complex social conditions that would otherwise normally result in rather mundane projects.

This is counter to the model of research that serves the needs of practice directly, but that gives some value to discussing the work of architecture with other disciplines. The reflexivity introduced by conducting an ethnographic project gives an architectural practice several opportunities to understand the inherent value of their practice's position, its studio culture and its working processes. This is one of the key ideas in Donald Schön's classic works on practice-based research.[4] The discussion with Dykers also touched on research questions:

> **CD:** Research suggests certainty. Or, at least it, implies the understanding of certainty. And how much 'certainty' has relevance is a question .... That's deeply philosophical.

RL: One of the questions that I am trying to get across is that research isn't so much to do with answers so much as having interesting questions.

CD: That's a good point, one of the next slides in [a recent lecture] was asking everyone, 'What is a concept?' One response is that a concept isn't an answer: it should always be a question. How can you have the right answer if you haven't asked the question. Just the other day I read a quote by Marshall McLuhan on that particular idea: if you start with the theory, you start with an answer. If you start with a concept, you start with a question.

It is worth reinforcing, once again, that research begins and ends with having good questions to ask: that answers are often partial and contingent, context dependent rather than absolute, and that this is more than OK; it is crucial to our understanding of the world not as a set of fixed conditions, but as variables that are in complex relationships with one another. Research is about questions, and these are pursued through conventional architectural practice as well as research-focused activities. Understanding design as an ongoing form of research is crucial to the development of architecture as a discipline, and the manifesto or position statement of a practice is one way of discussing this further:

RL: As an architect, I wonder if there is an overriding question that you want answered? Do you have a burning question in your work?

CD: The biggest question is twofold: 'What is architecture?' And I suppose in addition to that, 'If architecture isn't the end of the evolution of the built environment, what will replace architecture in the future?'

I think that those are interesting questions. We know that we make shelters, we make buildings and we make architecture. All of that has occurred in a couple of million years of development – and it's just hard to imagine that we are at the end of the line and we will never evolve any further. When will architecture be as passé as a building is to us today?

RL: I suppose from that, how do you go about finding out? Part of it is just to continue living.

CD: Again, if you look at the exercise of anthropological study, it is about what we are as human creatures, how we behave and how we evolve in terms of our own nakedness. And finally as we are realizing now, we are never truly naked because we always have some impact or relationship to our context that surrounds us.

For most of architectural history that context has been ignored to a certain degree. It may have been trivialized, or it may have been honoured in a kind of a way in which you might hold something up on a pedestal as untouchable. We have now realized that the world around us is very messy, and so are we. And that recognition is a way of seeing ourselves.

We are able to do that because science, which has changed us in the past is still doing that. So I think when we began to see the world as round – and the fact that it is round-ish is easily understood – it gave us a sense of superiority. But now that we see the world as just one small dot in a sea of something that we cannot even imagine or draw, because it is so fluid, our sense of superiority is shifting.

I suspect that in the future we will come to terms with this – and architecture will transform into something that is more system related and not just about objects.

Research in architecture is distinctively future-oriented, and looks towards what the discipline is, what it can be and what it needs to be. To that end, your research can contribute to the development of architecture – not as a static set of skills and interests that will gradually drop out of usefulness or fashion, but as the activities of an engaged and reflective practitioner who understands aspects of the world that they are a part of, and who has taken the time to develop an appropriate response to the conditions found there.[5] While technological research into materials or the latest forms of sustainable construction are undeniably valuable, there remains a need for architecture to respond to the history, society and culture it is a part of. These forms of research are no less important or demanding, and allow you to be a part of the changes and developments rather than a passive or reactive bystander.

Architectural research can reveal the interactions and entanglements between people and their environment, and the interactions and cultural values of building materials and construction technologies, suggesting ways forward and innovations in how to consider the material stuff of architecture. This offers the opportunity of discussing the degree of agency a building has over its users and vice versa, equipping you with a set of problems that are worlds away from the solid realities of Classical models of Western architecture.

Additionally, your activities as a researcher can give insights into the cognitive role of the built environment – not only how it affects our psychological states, but also how it can allow certain patterns of behaviour, certain ways of *being* in the world. Moving beyond simplistic distinctions between the intimacy of the home environment and the sterile control of institutional architecture, what lessons can be learnt from environmental psychology's assessment of architecture, and what propositions can be proffered, given the ability of architecture to alter mental states and emotions?

Architecture always occurs within a historical context, and while this is one of the most familiar paths for architectural research to take, it is one that offers further opportunities and ways of understanding. Our take on architectural history is always fresh, and filtered through the time at which we are writing. The Gothic now is not the same as it was in Pugin's time, and it would be inappropriate for us to build now as he did then. Historical architecture is a reference point that can and should be mobilized in your design practices, continually relevant to the present and offering precedents for close investigation.

The built environment cannot be other than political in nature. In common with other aspects of life, a complex set of often contradictory interests are at play in the construction of any project. More than merely the party politics of daily news reports, this political aspect of architecture asks difficult questions of the profession regarding aspects that are often out of the practitioner's control. This can include the large-scale politics of institutions such as building regulation and planning control, but also down to the implications of decorative styles, the question of who architecture is for, and the place of a structure within wider socio-economic circumstances. Architecture has a public, civic presence, and has the potential to be democratic.

Various strands of philosophy have informed architectural research over the last 100 years. This is not to write these interests off as mere fashion, but rather to understand that this interest has implications for what and how you design, as well as how you understand the buildings around you. Deconstruction, following a literary movement, asked serious questions about what the nature of architecture is. What is the role of the author in architecture, and how open is it to the alternative readings of one who dwells there? Phenomenological approaches consider our experience of the world in ways other than the absolute abstractions of geometry, and this collection of memory, association, sensoriality and temporality contribute to the unique feeling of a place.

Ethnographic research builds on models of interviewing, and asks architects to refrain from making assumptions in favour of actually finding out how people live, and what they think. This involves a respect for the group you are working with, and accepting that there is no single way of living, no norm to which we can or should all subscribe. This is a significant challenge, as it often asks for a methodological atheism, a methodological philistinism. Your own opinions are not important, as your research is about your informants as much as it can be.

It is worth concluding with the idea of what a distinctively *architectural* research might look like. Architecture has long been a discipline that looks out to others in order to find methods and ideas, but this can sometimes neglect the practice of architecture itself. Drawing, diagramming and other forms of graphic representation are an integral part of architectural *design*, and can be a similarly important aspect of architectural *research*, recasting your output as a conversation between writing and drawing, a collaboration between different modes of research that is appropriate to how architects practise. More than a guide to conducting architectural research, I hope that this book asks the question, 'What can an architectural research be?' The answers can be surprising, rigorous and, above all, useful in our understanding and design of the built environment.

Glossary

Analysis
The process of understanding and extracting the relevant information from a collection of data. Analysis could be said to be what you make out of your data: your conclusions.

Anthropology
One of the social sciences, anthropology considers the different ways people understand their lives. It is particularly good at challenging assumptions based upon our own lifestyles. It is one of the most fruitful areas for cross-disciplinary collaboration with architecture.

Aspirational architecture
The belief and intent that the built environment can improve lives.

Commodity status
A term from material culture studies, this status denotes the extent to which something belongs to an economic exchange. The nature of that belonging is referred to as its commodity status.

Critical discourse analysis
A methodology that assumes every form of cultural production includes a series of reflections upon the broader context within which it is produced. Critical discourse analysis seeks to analyze the underlying, hidden, or less obvious aspects of a cultural phenomenon.

Cross-sectional studies
Studies involving the collection of data from a defined population over a short or single period of time.

Cultural indicators
Outwardly visible signs of belonging to a given culture or society. These are often used deliberately to construct a sense of identity.

Dialectics
A philosophical method used to frame your research as a debate or discourse: presenting both sides of the argument in order to reason out a conclusion.

Dichotomy
Division or contrast. For example between the local and the global, or subjective and objective. This term is often problematized as a 'false dichotomy', where a spectrum of conditions is more appropriate.

Discipline
A field of expertise, an area of study, a discrete collection of practices, or all three. Working with other disciplines is referred to as cross-disciplinary or inter-disciplinary.

Emic
In studying how contemporary architecture operates in the world, the emic account is produced from within a culture. A street-level view of the built environment. See also *Etic*.

Enlightenment rationalism
The use of logic, reason and science to solve problems and gain understanding. This is often opposed to the Romantic tradition, which is more intuitive.

Entanglement
The belief that people and things are never isolated from one another, and must be approached as being co-dependent.

Environmental psychology
The study of how people engage with their environment, and what influence it has on them.

Ethnography
Exploration of people and cultures, looking at phenomena from the point of view of the subject. Attention is paid to what people say, how they say it, what they do, and how these differ. Ethnography is a research method that relies on field work, spending time in an environment with the people who live there.

Etic
In studying how contemporary architecture operates in the world, the etic account is from the point of view of an observer who is outside the culture or activity in question. A bird's-eye view of the built environment. See also *Emic*.

Inscriptive practices
The use of methods such as drawing, notation, cartography and diagrams to gain understanding of things. The process of making the drawing is prioritized here, rather than the analysis of material suggested by visual culture studies.

Longitudinal studies
Research studies involving observing the same variables over long periods of time.

Material culture
An approach to research that considers materials to have something important to tell us. Often discussed in terms of materials as having a biography or narrative that includes the practices by which they are extracted as raw materials and assembled as well as any cultural associations they may have.

Modernism
A multifaceted term that refers to a number of related movements across economics, politics, art and science. In architecture, this is associated with urbanization, industrialization, globalization, and new materials as well as an associated style of architecture with stripped back detailing and form which reflects the function of the scheme. This functionalism is critiqued in subsequent movements such as post-modernism or new urbanism.

People-environment studies
Related to environmental psychology, this is a multidisciplinary study devoted to understanding the multitude of ways in which we interact with our environment, and the effect that it has upon us.

Phenomenology
Studying the conscious experience of a phenomenon, the ways in which things manifest or appear to us as individuals. Phenomenology considers subjectivity to be not only unavoidable, but essential to understanding.

Procurement
The purchase of the raw material and the manner in which it is obtained, for example mined or farmed.

Restorative environments
Buildings and natural settings that aid healthy lifestyles and confer benefits such as recovery from tension or fatigue.

Sensory notation
A system for multi-sensory description of urban space with an aim of encouraging design for all our senses rather than a presumed visual bias.

Utopia
Often taken to mean an ideal place, but originally this term meant 'no-place' or 'any-place'. Utopian architecture is often bereft of context, of site, of location, and subsequently fails.

Vernacular architecture
Structures made without the intervention of professional architects, which have arisen out of a local tradition and led to the establishment of a local architectural language.

Endnotes

Introduction

1   Conventionally thought of as those academic disciplines that are concerned with culture and philosophy, crossing as far as anthropology – but crucially differentiated from science. More than one correct answer is possible to humanities disciplines, rather than the single correct answer sought by science.

2   It is worth noting that whilst 'data' is typically understood to mean statistical information sets, it can also be used to describe more subjective data: it is the raw material of your endeavours as a researcher.

3   See Pike, K. (Ed.). *Language in Relation to the Unified Theory of Structure of Human Behavior*, The Hague: Mouton, 1967.

4   Goodenough, W. 'Describing a Culture', *Description and Comparison in Cultural Anthropology*. Cambridge, Cambridge University Press, 1970. pp. 104–119.
Harris, M. 'The Epistemology of Cultural Materialism', *Cultural Materialism: The Struggle for a Science of Culture*. New York: Random House, 1980. pp. 29–45

5   Gould, P. & White, R. *Mental Maps*. London: Routledge, 1986.
Lynch, K. *The Image of the City*. Cambridge, Massachusetts: MIT Press, 1960.

6   Bergson, H. *Time and Free Will: an essay on the immediate data of consciousness*. New York: Dover Publications, 2001 [1889].
Tschumi, B. *The Manhattan Transcripts*. London: Academy Editions, 1994.

7   For an explicitly architectural understanding of this concept, see Smith, K. 'Debating a Discipline: Architecture, Argument and the Concept of the Dialectic' in *Introducing Architectural Theory: Debating a Discipline*. London: Routledge, 2012. pp.8-11 and subsequent chapters on Dialectical Readings in Architecture.

8   Key readings include, but are not restricted to the following:
Derrida, J. *Of Grammatology*. Baltimore: John Hopkins University Press, 1998.
Deleuze, G. *Difference & Repetition*. London: Bloomsbury, 2014.
Benjamin, W. *Illuminations*. London: Pimlico, 1999.
Heidegger, M. *Being and Time*. London: Blackwell, 1978.

9   See Tschumi, B. *The Manhattan Transcripts*. London: Academy Editions, 1994.
Eisenman, P. *House X*. New York: Rizzoli, 1982.

10   Tschumi, B. *Event-Cities*. Cambridge, Massachusetts: MIT Press, 1994.
Tschumi, B. *Architecture and Disjunction*. Cambridge, Massachusetts: MIT Press, 1996.

11   Eisenman, P. *Ten Canonical Buildings: 1950-2000*. New York: Rizzoli, 2008.

12   Appadurai, A (Ed.). 'Introduction: Commodities and the Politics of Value' in *The Social Life of Things: Commodities in Cultural Perspective*. Cambridge: Cambridge University Press, 1986. pp.3-63.
Hodder, I. *Entangled: An Archaeology of the Relationships Between Humans and Things*. London: John Wiley & Sons, 2012, p.3.
Buchli, V. 'Khrushchev, Modernism and the Fight Against Petit-Bourgeois Consciousness in the Soviet Home' in Buchli, V. (Ed.) *The Material Culture Reader*, Oxford: Berg, 2002. pp.207-236.

13   Tafuri, M. *Interpreting the Renaissance: Princes, Cities, Architects*. New Haven, Connecticut: Yale University Pres, 2006.
Rowe, C. *The Mathematics of the Ideal Villa and Other Essays*. Cambridge, Massachusetts: MIT Press, 1976.
Evans, R. *The Projective Cast: Architecture and its Three Geometries*. Cambridge, Massachuesetts: MIT Press, 2000.
Rkywert, J. *On Adam's House in Paradise: The Idea of the Primitive Hut in Architectural History*. Cambridge, Massachusetts: MIT Press, [1981] 1993.

14   Heidegger, M. *Being and Time*. London: Blackwell, 1978.
Merleau-Ponty, M. *The Phenomenology of Perception*. London: Routledge, 2002.

[15] Yaneva, A. *Made by the Office for Metropolitan Architecture: An Ethnography of Design*. Rotterdam: 010 Publishers, 2009.

Houdart, S. & M. Chihiro. *Kuma Kengo: An Unconventional Monograph*. Paris: Editions Donner Lieu, 2009.

Chapter 1

[1] Augé, M. *Non-Places: An Introduction to Supermodernity*. London: Verso Books, 2009.
[2] Lefebvre, H. *The Production of Space*. London: Wiley-Blackwell, 1991.
Foucault, M. *Discipline and Punish: The Birth of the Prison*. London: Penguin Books, 1991.
[3] Banham, R. *The Architecture of the Well-Tempered Environment*. Oxford: Architectural Press, 1969.
[4] Bollnow, O. F. *Human Space*. London: Hyphen Press, 2011.
[5] Ingold, T. *The Perception of the Environment*. London: Routledge, 2000.
[6] Gibson, J. J. *The Ecological Approach to Visual Perception*. London: Psychology Press, 1986.
[7] Casey, E. *The Fate of Place: A Philosophical History*. Berkeley: University of California Press, 2013.
Casey, E. *Getting Back into Place: Toward a Renewed Understanding of the Place-World*. Bloomington: Indiana University Press, 2009.
Casey, E. *Representing Place: Landscape Painting and Maps*. Ann Arbor: University of Minnesota Press, 2002.
[8] Isozaki, A. *Japan-ness in Architecture*. Cambridge, Massachusetts: MIT Press, 2006.
[9] Kuma, K. *Anti-Object*. London: Architectural Association, 2008.
[10] Venturi, R., D. Scott Brown & S. Izenour. *Learning from Las Vegas*. Cambridge, Massachusetts: MIT Press, 1972.

Chapter 2

[1] Gunn, W. *The Social and Environmental Impact of Incorporating Computer Aided Design Technology into an Architectural Design Process*. Unpublished PhD thesis, University of Manchester, 2002.
Yaneva, A. *The Making of a Building: A Pragmatist Approach to Architecture*. Berne: Peter Lang, 2009.
Landsverk Hagen, A. *Fear and Magic in Architects' Utopia: The Power of Creativity among the Snøhetta of Oslo and New York*. Unpublished PhD thesis, University of Oslo, 2014.
[2] Daniels, I. (author) & S. Andrews (photographer). *The Japanese House: Material Culture in the Modern Home*. Oxford: Berg, 2010.
[3] Black, R. *Porta Palazzo: The Anthropology of an Italian Market*. Philadelphia: University of Pennsylvania Press, 2012.
[4] Bestor, T. *Tsukiji: The Fish Market at the Center of the World*. Berkeley: University of California Press, 2004.
[5] Clifford, J. & G. Marcus (eds.). *Writing Culture: The Poetics and Politics of Ethnography*. Berkeley: University of California Press, 1992.
[6] Brunskill, R. W. *Vernacular Architecture: An Illustrated Handbook*. London: Faber & Faber, 2000.
Glassie, H. *Vernacular Architecture*. Bloomington: Indiana University Press, 2000.
[7] Le Corbusier. *Towards a New Architecture*. London: Butterworth, [1923] 1989.
[8] Sullivan, L. *The Tall Office Building Artistically Considered*. Getty Research Institute, 1896. https://archive.org/details/tallofficebuildi00sull (accessed 29 November 2014).
[9] Schön, D. *The Reflective Practitioner: How Professionals Think in Action*. New York: Basic Books, 1984
[10] Kellein, T. & J. Hendricks (eds.). *Fluxus*. London: Thames & Hudson, 1995.

Chapter 3

[1] Aitken, I. *The Documentary Film Movement: An Anthology*. Edinburgh: Edinburgh University Press, 1998.

Chapter 4

[1] Adorno, T. *Aesthetic Theory*. London: Bloomsbury, [1970] 2013. DeNora, T. *After Adorno: Rethinking Music Sociology*. Cambridge: Cambridge University Press, 2003.
[2] Eisenstein, S. *Film Form: Essays in Film Theory*. New York: Mariner Books, [1949] 2014.
[3] Ricoeur, P. *The Rule of Metaphor: The Creation of Meaning in Language*. London: Routledge, 2003.

Chapter 5

[1] A deeper investigation of the field notes themselves is contained in Gunn, W. (ed.). *Fieldnotes and Sketchbooks: Challenging the Boundaries Between Descriptions and Processes of Describing.* Berne: Peter Lang, 2009.

[2] Further reading includes the following:

Heinrich, M. *Basics: Architectural Photography.* Berlin: Birkhäuser, 2008.

Kopelow, G. *How to Photograph Buildings and Interiors.* Princeton: Princeton Architectural Press, 2002.

Caiger-Smith, M. & D. Chandler. *Site Work: Architecture in Photography Since Early Modernism.* London: Photographers' Gallery, 1991.

[3] Shulz, A. *Architectural Photography: Composition, Capture, and Digital Image Processing.* Santa Barbara, California: Rocky Nook, 2012.

Pardo, A., E. Redstone & D. Campany. *Constructing Worlds: Photography and Architecture in the Modern World.* Munich: Prestel, 2014.

Redstone, E., P. Gadanho & K. Bush. *Shooting Space: Architecture in Contemporary Photography.* London: Phaidon Press, 2014.

Hausenberg, A. & A. Simons. *Architectural Photography: Construction and Design Manual.* Berlin: Jovis Verlag, 2012.

Chapter 6

[1] Taking Manchester as an example, your starting point would be with the Royal Institute of British Architects (RIBA) North West, the official body representing architects in the region. Further societies such as the Manchester Society of Architects run parallel events that are not related to the legislative function of the RIBA. More informal still are groups such as Urban Sketchers Manchester, the Manchester Modernist Society or the Manchester Salon. Student associations such as the Manchester Student Society of Architecture and Before You're 30 offer great networking that cuts across the different stages of architectural education and the profession. This is supplemented by initiatives such as Cities@ Manchester and its events, run from the University of Manchester and relating to a wide range of disciplines, including architecture, planning, geography and development studies. Every major city will have similar organizations – or where they do not, it is worth establishing your own meetings in order to build a network that is mutually beneficial.

[2] Lynch, K. *The Image of the City.* Cambridge, Massachusetts: MIT Press, 1960.

Chapter 8

[1] Appadurai, A. 'Commodities and the Politics of Value', in *The Social Life of Things: Commoditites in Cultural Perspective.* Cambridge: Cambridge University Press, 1986, pp.3–63

Mauss, M. *The Gift: Forms and Functions of Exchange in Archaic Societies* London: Routledge, [1954] 2002.

[2] Appadurai, A. 'Commodities and the Politics of Value', p.13.

[3] *Ibid.*

[4] *Ibid.,* p.15.

[5] *Ibid.*

[6] It is worth noting that it is not often noticeably quicker for the customer to use an automated system, but that it makes economic sense as human staff on ticket desks are comparatively costly.

[7] *Ibid.,* p.56.

[8] *Ibid.,* p.57.

[9] Hodder, I. *Entangled: An Archaeology of the Relationships Between Humans and Things.* London: John Wiley & Sons, 2012, p.3.

[10] See also:

Cairns, S. & J. M. Jacobs. *Buildings Must Die: a Perverse View of Architecture.* Cambridge, Massachusetts: MIT Press, 2014.

Van der Hoorne, M. *Indispensable Eyesores: an Anthropology of Undesired Buildings.* New York: Berghahn Books, 2009.

[11] Küchler, S. *Malanggan: Art, Memory and Sacrifice.* Oxford: Berg, 2002.

[12] Gell, A. *Art and Agency: An Anthropological Theory.* Oxford: Clarendon Press, 1998.

[13] Miller, D. *Stuff.* Cambridge: Polity Press, 2010.

[14] Buchli, V. 'Khrushchev, Modernism and the Fight Against Petit-Bourgeois Consciousness in the Soviet Home', in *The Material Culture Reader.* Oxford: Berg, 2002, pp.207–36.

[15] Belardi, P. *Why Architects Still Draw*. Cambridge, Massachusetts: MIT Press, 2014, p.90.

[16] Novak, Z. Translator's note in *Ibid.*, pp.x–xi.

Chapter 9

[1] Other allied associations and organizations include the Environmental Behaviour Research Association, which has a strong geographic basis in East Asia; and the Environmental Design Research Association, which has a more direct design agenda.

[2] Thwaites, K., S. Porta, O. Romice & M. Greaves (eds.). *Urban Sustainability Through Environmental Design: Approaches to Time-People-Place Responsive Urban Spaces*. London: Taylor & Francis, 2007.
Thwaites, K. & I. Simkins. *Experiential Landscape: An Approach to People, Place and Space*. London: Routledge, 2007.

[3] Chion, M. *The Voice in Cinema*. New York: Columbia University Press, 1999.

[4] Coyne, R. *Technoromanticism: Digital Narrative, Holism, and the Romance of the Real*. Cambridge, Massachusetts: MIT Press, 2001.

[5] Barthes, R. *Image, Music, Text*. New York: Fontana Press, [1977] 1993, p.181.

[6] Tuan, Yi-Fu, *Space and Place: The Perspective of Experience*. Ann Arbor: University of Minnesota Press, 1977, p.15.

[7] Barthes, R. 'The Grain of the Voice', in *Image, Music, Text*, pp.179–89.

Chapter 10

[1] Akutagawa, Ryunosuke. 'Rashomon' and 'In a Bamboo Grove', in Rubin, J. (trans.), *Rashomon and Seventeen Other Stories*. London: Penguin Books, 2006.

[2] Tafuri, M. *Architecture and Utopia: Design and Capitalist Development*. Cambridge, Massachusetts: MIT Press, 1976.
Tafuri, M. *Interpreting the Renaissance: Princes, Cities, Architects*. New Haven, Connecticut: Yale University Press, 2006.
Tafuri, M. *Venice and the Renaissance*. Cambridge, Massachusetts: MIT Press, 1995.
Tafuri, M. *Theories and History of Architecture*. Cambridge, Massachusetts: MIT Press, 1981.

[3] Tafuri, *Interpreting the Renaissance*, p.xi.

[4] Moore, T. *Utopia*. London: Penguin Books, [1516] 2012.

[5] Nesbitt, K. (ed.). *Theorizing a New Agenda for Architecture: Anthology of Architectural Theory 1965–1995*. Princetone: Princeton Architectural Press, 1996, p.360.

[6] Rowe, C. *The Mathematics of the Ideal Villa and Other Essays*. Cambridge, Massachusetts: MIT Press, 1976.
Rowe, C. & F. Koetter. *Collage City*. Cambridge, Massachusetts: MIT Press, 1978

[7] Evans, R. *Translations from Drawing to Building and Other Essays*. London: Architectural Association, 1996.

[8] Evans, R. *The Projective Cast: Architecture and its Three Geometries*. Cambridge, Massachusetts: MIT Press, 2000, p.xxvii.

[9] Rkywert, J. *On Adam's House in Paradise: The Idea of the Primitive Hut in Architectural History*. Cambridge, Massachusetts: MIT Press, [1981] 1993.

[10] *Ibid.*, p.183.

[11] Rkywert, J. *The Dancing Column: On Order in Architecture*. Cambridge, Massachusetts: MIT Press, 1998.

[12] Rkywert, J. *The Judicious Eye: Architecture Against the Other Arts*. Cambridge, Massachusetts: MIT Press, 2008.

[13] Published by Yale University Press, a wide range of such guides are now in print as revised versions of Pevsner's initial work, or new scholarship in the tradition of Pevsner's model.

[14] Pevsner, N. *An Outline of European Architecture*. London: Thames & Hudson, 2009.
Pevsner, N. *Visual Planning and the Picturesque*. Los Angeles: Getty Research Institute, 2010.

[15] Pevsner, *An Outline of European Architecture*, p.10.

[16] Pevsner, *Visual Planning and the Picturesque*, p.10.

[17] A wealth of sources are available on this, including:
Benton, T., C. Benton & D. Sharp (eds.). *Form and Function: A Source Book for the History of Architecture and Design 1890–1939*. London: Crosby Lockwood Staples/ Open University Press, 1975.
Conrads, U. (ed.). *Programs and Manifestoes on 20th-Century Architecture*. Cambridge, Massachusetts: MIT Press, 1971.

Danchev, A. (ed.). *100 Artist' Manifestos: From the Futurists to the Stuckists*. London: Penguin Books, 2011.

Hughes, J. & S. Sadler (eds.). *Non-Plan: Essays on Freedom, Participation and Change in Architecture and Urbanism*. Oxford: Architectural Press, 1999.

Jencks, C. & K. Kropf (eds.). *Theories and Manifestoes of Contemporary Architecture*. London: Academy Editions, 1997.

[18] Le Corbusier. *Towards a New Architecture*. London: Butterworth, [1923] 1989.

[19] Le Corbusier, *Towards a New Architecture*, p.35.

[20] Loos, A. *Ornament and Crime*. Riverside, California: Ariadne Press, 1998.

[21] Le Corbusier, *Towards a New Architecture*, p.45.

[22] *Ibid.*, p.51.

[23] *Ibid.*, p.87.

[24] Pai, H. *The Portfolio and the Diagram*. Cambridge, Massachusetts: MIT Press, 2002.

[25] Bergson, H. *The Creative Mind: An Introduction to Metaphysics*. Andison, M. L. (trans.), New York: Citadel Press, 1992, p.100.

[26] *Ibid.*, p.21.

[27] Le Corbusier, *Towards a New Architecture*, p.107.

Chapter 11

[1] Lefebvre, H. *Writings on Cities*. London: Wiley-Blackwell, 1995.

[2] Orwell, G. 'Politics and the English Language', in *Why I Write*. London: Penguin Books, 1994, p.116.

[3] Lefebvre, H. *The Critique of Everyday Life*. London: Verso Books, 2014.
Lefebvre, H. *The Production of Space*. London: Wiley-Blackwell, 1991.

[4] Harvey, D. *Rebel Cities: From the Right to the City to the Urban Revolution*. London: Verso Books, 2013.
Harvey, D. *The Condition of Postmodernity*. London: Wiley-Blackwell, 1991.

[5] See also:
Bourdieu, P. *The Logic of Practice*. Cambridge: Polity Press, [1980] 1990.
De Certeau, M. *The Practice of Everyday Life*. Berkeley: University of California Press, 1984.

[6] Lefebvre, *The Practice of Everyday Life*, pp.30–31.

[7] *Ibid,*. p.68.

[8] Debord, G. *The Society of the Spectacle*. New York: Zone Books, [1967] 1994, p.120.

[9] For an architectural discussion of this movement, the following texts are helpful:
Sadler, S. *The Situationist City*. Cambridge, Massachusetts: MIT Press, 1998.
Wigley, M. *Constant's New Babylon: The Hyper-Architecture of Desire*. Rotterdam: 010 Publishers, 1998.
De Zegher, C. & M. Wigley (eds.). *The Activist Drawing: Retracing Situationist Architectures from Constant's New Babylon to Beyond*. Cambridge, Massachusetts: MIT Press and the Drawing Center, New York, 2001.

[10] Debord, *The Society of the Spectacle*, pp.122–23.

[11] Gould, P. & R. White. *Mental Maps*. London: Routledge, 1986.
Lynch, K. *The Image of the City*. Cambridge, Massachusetts: MIT Press, 1960.

[12] Aitken, I. *Film and Reform: John Grierson and the Documentary Film Movement*. London: Routledge, 1992.

Chapter 12

[1] Venturi, R., D. Scott Brown & S. Izenour. *Learning From Las Vegas*. Cambridge, Massachusetts: MIT Press, [1972] 1997.

[2] *Ibid.*, p.87.

[3] *Ibid.*

[4] *Ibid.*, pp.52–53.

[5] Tschumi, B. *Architecture and Disjunction*. Cambridge, Massachusetts: MIT Press, 1996, pp.191–92.

[6] *Ibid.*, p.204.

[7] Heidegger, M. *Being and Time*. London: Blackwell, 1978.
Heidegger's legacy remains tainted by his association with the Nazi Party in 1930s Germany, so it is worth remaining mindful of this association, particularly when reading passages about the importance of place.

8 Sharr, A. *Heidegger for Architects*. London, Routledge, 2007.

9 Heidegger, M. 'Building Dwelling Thinking', in Farrell Krell, D. (ed.), *Basic Writings: Martin Heidegger*. London: Routledge, [1978] 1993, pp. 344–63.

10 *Ibid.*, 347.

11 Sharr, A. *Heidegger for Architects*. London: Routledge, 2007.

12 Merleau-Ponty, M. *The Phenomenology of Perception*. London: Routledge, 2002, p.ix.

13 *Ibid.*, p.vii.

14 *Ibid.*, p.9.

15 *Ibid.*, p.7.

16 Gibson, J. J. *The Ecological Approach to Visual Perception*. London: Psychology Press, 1986.
Gibson, J. J. *The Senses Considered as Perceptual Systems*. Westport, Connecticut: Greenwood Press, 1983.

17 Gibson, *The Senses Considered as Perceptual Systems*, p.33.

18 Ingold, T. *The Perception of the Environment: Essays in Livelihood, Dwelling and Skill*. London: Routledge, 2000.

19 Calvino, I. *Under the Jaguar Sun*. London: Penguin Books, 2001, p.58.
For more on the use of literature in architecture, see Charley, J. *Memories of Cities: Trips and Manifestoes*. Farnham: Ashgate, 2013.

20 Lucas, R, G. Mair & O. Romice. 'Making Sense of the City: Representing the Multi-Modality of Urban Space', in Inns, T. (ed.), *Designing for the 21st Century: Interdisciplinary Methods & Findings*. Farnham: Ashgate, 2009.

21 Lynch, K. *The Image of the City*. Cambridge, Massachusetts: MIT Press, 1960.
Cullen, G. *The Concise Townscape*. London: Architectural Press, 1961.
Gandelsonas, M. *X-Urbanism: Architecture and the American City*. Princeton: Princeton Architectural Press, 1999.
Thiel, P. *People, Paths, and Purposes: Notations for a Participatory Envirotecture*. Seattle: University of Washington Press, 1997.

22 Laban, R & F. C. Lawrence. *Effort*. London: Macdonald & Evans Ltd, 1979.

23 Lucas, R. *Sensory Notation Handbook*. Manchester: Flâneur Press, and lulu.com, 2014.

Chapter 13

1 Emerson, R. M. *Writing Ethnographic Fieldnotes*. University of Chicago Press, 1995.
Van Maanen, J. *Tale of the Field: on Writing Ethnography*. University of Chicago Press, 1988.
Atkinson, P. A., Delamont, S. & Coffey, A. (Eds.). *Handbook of Ethnography*. Sage Publications, 2007.

2 Clifford, J. & Marcus, G. (Eds.) *Writing Culture*. Berkeley: University of California Press, 1992.

3 Dawson, A., Hockey, J. & James, A. (Eds.). *After Writing Culture*. London: Routledge, 1997.

4 Bestor, T. *Tsukiji: The Fish Market at the Center of the World*. Berkeley: University of California Press, 2004.

5 Black, R. E. *Porta Palazzo: The Anthropology of an Italian Market*. Philadelphia: University of Pennsylvania Press, 2012.

6 de la Pradelle, M. *Market Day in Provence*. University of Chicago Press, 2006.

7 Daniels, I. (Author) & Andrews, S. (Photographer) *The Japanese Home: Material Culture in the Modern Home*. Oxford: Berg, 2010.

8 Pink, S. *Home Truths: Gender, Domestic Objects and Everyday Life*. Oxford: Berg, 2004.

9 Reed-Danahay (Ed.). *Auto/Ethnography: Rewriting the Self and the Social*. Oxford: Berg, 1997.

10 Meneley, A. & Young, D. (Eds.). *Auto-ethnographies: The Anthropology of Academic Practices*. Broadview Press, 2005.

11 Lucas, R. *Filmic Architecture: an exploration of film language as a method for architectural criticism and design*. Unpublished MPhil by Research, Glasgow: University of Strathclyde, 2002.

12 Laban movement notation is a codified form of dance notation with particularly interesting features, most significantly its focus on the efforts required by the dancer rather than the form made by the body.

13 Gunn, W. (Ed.). *Creativity and Practice Research Papers: A Series of Publications Exploring the Interfaces Between the Knowledge Traditions of Fine Art, Architecture and Anthropology*. Dundee: Creativity and Practice Research Group, 2005.

14 Lucas, R. 'Gestural Artefacts: Notations of a Daruma Doll.' in Gunn, W (Ed.). *Fieldnotes and Sketchbooks: Challenging the Boundaries Between Descriptions and Processes of Describing*. Peter Lang Publishers, 2009.

Chapter 14

[1] Woods, L. *War and Architecture*. Princeton: Princeton Architectural Press, 1996.

Tschumi, B. *The Manhattan Transcripts*. London: Academy Editions, 1994.

Evans, R. 1984. 'In Front of Lines That Leave Nothing Behind', in Hays, K.M. (ed.). *Architecture Theory Since 1968*. Cambridge, Massachusetts: MIT Press, 2000.

Hejduk, J. *Adjusting Foundations*. New York: Monacelli Press, 1995.

Hejduk, J. *Victims*. London: Architectural Association, 1986.

[2] Eisenman, P. *The Formal Basis of Modern Architecture*. Zurich: Lars Müller Publishers, [1973] 2006.

Eisenman, P. *Ten Canonical Buildings: 1950-2000*. New York: Rizooli, 2008.

[3] Unwin, S. *Analysing Architecture*. London: Routledge, 2003, p.15.

[4] *Ibid.*

[5] *Ibid.*, p.18.

[6] Gunn, W. (ed.). *Fieldnotes and Sketchbooks: Challenging the Boundaries Between Descriptions and Processes of Describing*. Berne: Peter Lang, 2009, p.37.

[7] Lucas, R. 'Taking a Line for a Walk: Walking as an Aesthetic Practice', in Ingold, T. & J. L. Vergunst (eds.) *Ways of Walking: Ethnography and Practice on Foot*. Farnham: Ashgate, 2008.

Lucas, R. 'Getting Lost in Tokyo' in *Footprint*, Delft School of Design journal, Issue 2, 2008. www.footprintjournal.org

[8] Hutchinson-Guest, A. *Choreo-Graphics: A Comparison of Dance Notation Systems From the Fifteenth Century to the Present*. Amsterdam: Gordon and Breach, 1989.

Kipling Brown, A. & M. Parker. *Dance Notation for Beginners: Labanotation, Benesh Movement Notation*. London: Dance Books, 1984.

Laban, R. *The Language of Movement: A Guidebook to Choreutics*. Boston: Plays Inc, 1966.

Laban, R. & L. Ullman. *The Mastery of Movement*. London: Macdonald & Evans Ltd, 1971.

[9] Lang, P. & W. Menking. *Superstudio: Life Without Objects*. Milan: Skira Editore, 2003.

[10] Gell, A. 'Vogel's Net: Traps as Artworks and Artworks as Traps', in *Journal of Material Culture*, 1996, Volume 1, p.15. http://mcu.sagepub.com/content/1/1/15

Deleuze, G. *Cinema 2: The Time-Image*. London: Athlone Press, 1994.

Chapter 15

[1] Adam, R. *The Globalisation of Modern Architecture: The Impact of Politics, Economics and Social Change on Architecture and Urban Design Since 1990*. Newcastle upon Tyne: Cambridge Scholars Publishing, 2013.

The firm's website lists a number of their publications and reports: www.adamarchitecture.com/publications/articles-papers.htm

[2] Hillier, B. & J. Hanson. *The Social Logic of Space*. Cambridge: Cambridge University Press, 1989.

Porta, S. & O. Romice. *Plot-Based Urbanism: Towards Time-Consciousness in Place-Making*. Glasgow: University of Strathclyde, 2010.

http://strathprints.strath.ac.uk/35640/1/Plot_Based_Urbanism_10_OR_SP_FINAL_low_res.pdf

[3] Gunn, W. *The Social and Environmental Impact of Incorporating Computer Aided Design Technology into an Architectural Design Process*. Unpublished PhD thesis, University of Manchester, 2002.

Landsverk Hagen, A. *Fear and Magic in Architects' Utopia: The Power of Creativity Among the Snøhetta, of Oslo and New York*. Unpublished PhD thesis, University of Oslo, 2014.

[4] Douglas, A., Coessens, K. & Crispin, D. *The Artistic Turn: A Manifesto (Orpheus Research Centre in Music Series)*. Leuven University Press, 2009.

Gray, C. *Visualising Research: A Guide to Research Process in Art and Design*. Farnham: Ashgate, 2004.

[5] Schön, D. *The Reflective Practitioner: How Professionals Think in Action*. New York: Basic Books, 1984.

Bibliography

Adam, R. *The Globalisation of Modern Architecture: the Impact of Politics, Economics and Social Change on Architecture and Urban Design Since 1990.* Cambridge Scholars Publishing, 2013.

Adorno, T. *Aesthetic Theory.* London: Bloomsbury, 2013 [1970].

Appadurai, A. (Ed.) *The Social Life of Things.* Cambridge: Cambridge University Press, 1986.

Atkinson, P. A., Delamont, S. & Coffey, A. (Eds.). *Handbook of Ethnography.* Sage Publications, 2007.

Augé, M. *Non-Place: Introduction to an Anthropology of Supermodernity.* London: Verso Books, 2009.

Banham, R. *Los Angeles: The Architecture of Four Ecologies.* University of California Press, 2009.

Banham, R. *The Architecture of the Well Tempered Environment.* Oxford: The Architectural Press, 1969.

Banham, R. *Theory and Design in the First Machine Age.* Cambridge, Massachusetts: MIT Press, 1980.

Barthes, R. *Image, Music, Text.* New York: Fontana Press, 1971.

Baudrillard, J. *Simulacra & Simulation.* Michigan: University of Michigan Press, 1994.

Belardi, P. *Why Architects Still Draw.* Cambridge, Massachusetts: MIT Press, 2014.

Benjamin, W. *Illuminations.* London: Pimlico, 1999.

Benton, T., Benton, C. & Sharp, D. (Eds.), *Form and Function: A Source Book for the History of Architecture and Design 1890-1939.* London: Crosby Lockwood Staples/ Open University Press, 1975.

Bergson, H. *The Creative Mind: An Introduction to Metaphysics.* Andison, M. L. Trans. New York: Citadel Press, 1992.

Bergson, H. *Time and Free Will: an essay on the immediate data of consciousness.* New York: Dover Publications, 2001 [1889].

Bollnow, O.F. *Of Human Space.* London: Hyphen Press, 2011.

Bourdieu, P. *The Logic of Practice.* Cambridge: Polity Press, 1990[1980].

Brunskill, R.W. *Vernacular Architecture: an Illustrated Handbook.* London: Faber & Faber, 2000.

Buchli, V. 'Khrushchev, Modernism and the Fight Against Petit-Bourgeois Consciousness in the Soviet Home' in Buchli, V. (Ed.) 2002. The *Material Culture Reader*, pp.207-236. Oxford: Berg, 2002.

Buchli, V. *An Archaeology of Socialism.* Oxford: Berg, 2000.

Cairns, S. & Jacobs, J.M. *Buildings Must Die: a Perverse View of Architecture.* Cambridge, Massachusetts: MIT Press, 2014.

Canizaro, V.B. *Architectural Regionalism: Collected Writings on Place, Identity, Modernity and Tradition.* Princeton Architectural Press, 2006.

Casey, E. *Representing Place: Landscape Painting and Maps.* University of Minnesota Press, 2002.

Casey, E. *Getting Back into Place: Toward a Renewed Understanding of the Place-World.* Indiana University Press, 2009.

Casey, E. *The Fate of Place: a Philosophical History.* University of California Pres, 2013.

Charley, J. *Memories of Cities: Trips and Manifestoes.* Farnham: Ashgate, 2013.

Chion, M. *Voice in Cinema.* Columbia University Press, 1999.

Clifford, J. & Marcus, G. (Eds.)*Writing Culture.* Berkeley: University of California Press, 1992.

Conrads, Ulrich (Ed.). *Programs and Manifestoes on 20th Century Architecture.* Cambridge, Massachusetts: MIT Press, 1971.

Curtis, W. *Modern Architecture Since 1900.* London: Phaidon Press, 1990.

Danchev, Alex (Ed.). *100 Artist' Manifestos from the Futurists to the Stuckists.* London: Penguin, 2011.

Daniels, I. (Author) & Andrews, S. (Photographer) *The Japanese Home: Material Culture in the Modern Home.* Oxford: Berg, 2010.

Dawson, A., Hockey, J. & James, A. (Eds.). *After Writing Culture.* London: Routledge, 1997.

De Certeau, M. *The Practice of Everyday Life.* Berkeley & Los Angeles: University of California Press, 1984.

Debord, G. *The Society of the Spectacle.* New York: Zone Books, 1994 [1968].

Deleuze, G.*Cinema 2: The Time Image.* London: Athlone Press, 1994.

Deleuze, G. *Difference & Repetition.* London: Bloomsbury, 2014.

DeNora, T. *After Adorno: Rethinking Music Sociology.* Cambridge University Press, 2003.

Derrida, J. *Of Grammatology.* Baltimore: John Hopkins University Press, 1998.

Eisenman, P. *Ten Canonical Buildings.* New York: Rizzoli, 2008.

Eisenman, P. *House X.* New York: Rizzoli, 1982.

Eisenman, P. *The Formal Basis of Modern Architecture.* Lars Muller Publishers, 2006 [1963].

Eisenstein, S. *Film Form: Essays in Film Theory.* Mariner Books, 2014 [1949].

Emerson, R. M. *Writing Ethnographic Fieldnotes.* University of Chicago Press, 1995.

Evans, R. 'In Front of Lines That Leave Nothing Behind' in Hays, K.M. (Ed.). *Architecture Theory Since 1968.* Columbia University Press, 1984.

Evans, R. *Translations from Drawing to Building and Other Essays.* London: Architectural Association, 1996.

Evans, R. *The Projective Cast: Architecture and its Three Geometries.* Cambridge, Massachusetts: MIT Press, 2000.

Foucault, M. *Discipline and Punish: the Birth of the Prison.* London: Penguin Books, 1991.

Frampton, K. *Studies in Tectonic Culture: The Poetics of Construction in Nineteenth and Twentieth Century Architecture.* Cambridge, Massachusetts: MIT Press, 2001.

Frampton, K. *Labour, Work, Architecture: Collected Essays on Architecture and Design.* London: Routledge, 2002.

Gehl, J. *How to Study Public Life: Methods in Urban Design.* Island Press, 2013.

Gell, A. *Art and Agency: An Anthropological Theory.* Oxford: Clarendon Press, 1998.

Gibson, J. J. *The Senses Considered as Perceptual Systems.* Westport, Connecticut: Greenwood Press, 1983.

Gibson, J. J. *The Ecological Approach to Visual Perception.* Westport, Connecticut: Greenwood Press, 1986.

Glassie, H. *Vernacular Architecture.* Indiana University Press, 2000.

Goodenough, W. 'Describing a Culture', Description and Comparison in Cultural Anthropology. Cambridge, Cambridge University Press, 1970. pp. 104–119.

Gould, P. & White, R. *Mental Maps*. London: Routledge, 1984.

Gray, C. *Visualising Research: A Guide to Research Process in Art and Design*. Farnham: Ashgate, 2004.

Gunn, S. & Faire, L. (Eds.). *Research Methods for History*. Edinburgh: Edinburgh University Press, 2011.

Gunn, W. (Ed.). *Creativity and Practice Research Papers: A Series of Publications Exploring the Interfaces Between the Knowledge Traditions of Fine Art, Architecture and Anthropology*. Dundee: Creativity and Practice Research Group, 2005.

Gunn, W. & Donovan, J. (Eds.). *Design and Anthropology (Anthropological Studies of Creativity and Perception)*. Farnham: Ashgate, 2012.

Gunn, W., Otto, T. & Smith, R. C. (Eds.). *Design Anthropology: Theory and Practice*. London: Bloomsbury, 2013.

Gunn, W. *The social and environmental impact of incorporating computer aided design technology into an architectural design process*. Unpublished PhD thesis, University of Manchester, 2002.

Gunn, Wendy (Ed.) *Fieldnotes and Sketchbooks*. Peter Lang Books, 2009.

Harris, M. 'The Epistemology of Cultural Materialism', *Cultural Materialism: The Struggle for a Science of Culture*. New York: Random House, 1980. pp. 29–45

Harvey, D. *The Condition of Postmodernity*. London: Wiley-Blackwell, 1991.

Harvey, D. *Rebel Cities: from the Right to the City to the Urban Revolution*. London: Verso Books, 2013.

Hausenberg, A. & Simons, A. *Architectural Photography: Construction and Design Manual*. Jovis Verlag, 2012.

Hays, K.M. (Ed.). *Architectural Theory Since 1968*. Cambridge, Massachusetts: MIT Press, 2000.

Heidegger, M. (author) Farrell Krell, D (Ed.), 'Building Dwelling Thinking' in *Basic Writings*. London: Routledge, 1993[1978]. pp. 344-363.

Heidegger, M. 1978. *Being and Time*. London: Blackwell.

Heinrich, M. 2008. *Basics: Architectural photography*. Berlin: Birkha user.

Hillier, B. & Hanson, J. *The Social Logic of Space*. Cambridge University Press, 1989.

Hodder, I. *Entangled: an Archaeology of the Relationships Between Humans and Things*. London: John Wiley & Sons, 2012.

Houdart, S. *Kuma Kengo: an Unconventional Monograph*. Paris: Editions Donner Lieu, 2009.

Hughes, Jonathan & Sadler, Simon (Eds.). *Non-Plan: Essays on Freedom, Participation and Change in Architecture and Urbanism*. Oxford: The Architectural Press, 1999.

Hutchinson-Guest, A. *Choreo-Graphics: A Comparison of Dance Notation Systems From the Fifteenth Century to the Present*. Amsterdam: Gordon and Breach, 1989.

Ingold, T. *The Perception of the Environment: Essays in Livelihood, Dwelling and Skill*. London: Routledge, 2000.

Ingold, T. *Lines: A Brief History*. London: Routledge, 2007.

Ingold, T. *Making: Anthropology Archaeology, Art & Architecture*. London: Routledge, 2013.

Ingold, T. with R Lucas. 'The 4 A's (Anthropology, Archaeology, Art and Architecture): Reflections on a Teaching and Learning Experience.' in Harris, M (Ed.) *Ways of Knowing: New Approaches in the Anthropology of Knowledge and Learning.*, Oxford: Berhgahn Books, 2007.

Isozaki, A. *Japan-ness in Architecture*. Cambridge, Massachusetts: MIT Press, 2006.

Jencks, Charles & Kropf, Karl (Eds.). *Theories and Manifestoes of Contemporary Architecture*. Academy Editions, 1997.

Kipling Brown, A. with M Parker. *Dance Notation for Beginners: Labanotation, Benesh Movement Notation*. London: Dance Books, 1984.

Kopelow, G. *How to photograph buildings and interiors*. New York: Princeton Architectural Press, 2002.

Kuma, K. *Anti-Object*. London: Architectural Association, 2008.

Laaksonen, E., Simons, T. & Vartola, A. (Eds.). *Research and Practice in Architecture*. Helsinki: Rakennustieto Publishing, 1999.

Laban, R. *The language of Movement: A Guidebook to Choreutics*. Boston: Plays Inc, 1966.

Laban, R. & Ullman, L. *The Mastery of Movement*. London: Macdonald & Evans Ltd., 1971.

Landsverk Hagen, A. *Fear and magic in Architect's Utopia: The Power of Creativity among the Snøhettas of Oslo and New York*. Unpublished PhD thesis, University of Oslo, 2014.

Lang, P. & Menking, W. *Superstudio: Life Without Objects*. Skira Editore, 2003.

Le Corbusier. *Towards a New Architecture*. Butterworth, 1989 [1923].

Leach, A. *What is Architectural History?* Polity Press, 2010.

Lefaivre, L. & Tzonis, A. *Architectural Regionalism in the Age of Globalisation: Peaks and Valleys in the Flat World*. London: Routledge, 2011.

Lefebvre, H. *The Production of Space*. London: Wiley-Blackwell, 1991.

Lefebvre, H. *Writings on Cities*. London: Wiley-Blackwell, 1995.

Lefebvre, H. *The Critique of Everyday Life*. London: Verso Books, 2014.

Loos, A. *Ornament and Crime*. Ariadne Press, 1998.

Lucas, R & Romice, O. 'Representing Sensory Experience in Urban Design' in *Design Principles and Practices: an International Journal*. Volume 2, Issue 4, pp.83-94. Common Ground Publishers, 2008.

Lucas, R; Mair, G & Romice, O. 'Making Sense of the City: Representing the Multi-modality of Urban Space' in Inns, T. (Ed.), *Designing for the 21st Century: Interdisciplinary Methods & Findings*. Ashgate, 2009.

Lucas, R. 'Inscribing the City: A Flâneur in Tokyo'. *Anthropology Matters special issue: Cities*, 2004. www.anthropologymatters.com

Lucas, R. 'Getting Lost in Tokyo', in Gunn, W. Ed. *Creativity and Practice Research Papers*. Dundee: Centre for Artists Books / Creativity & Practice Research Group, 2005.

Lucas, R. 'Taking a Line for a Walk: Flânerie, Drifts, and the Artistic Potential of Urban Wandering.' in Ingold, T & Lee Vergunst, J (Eds.) *Ways of Walking: Ethnography and Practice on Foot*, Ashgate, 2008a.

Lucas, R. 'Getting Lost in Tokyo' in *Footprint*, Delft School of Design Journal, Issue 2, 2008a. www.footprintjournal.org/issues/current

Lucas, R. 'Acousmêtric Architecture: Filmic Sound Design and its Lessons for Architects' in *City in Film: Architecture, Urban Space and the Moving Image Conference Proceedings*, 2008c. University of Liverpool,

Lucas, R. 'Chion's Acousmêtre in Transit Space' in Bunn, S. (Ed.), *Sound & Anthropology*, 2008d. University of St Andrews. www.st-andrews.ac.uk/soundanth/work/lucas/

Lucas, R. 'The Sensory Experience of Sacred Space: Senso-Ji and Meiji-Jingu, Tokyo' in *MONU: Magazine on Urbanism*. Issue 10: Holy Urbanism, pp.46-55. Rotterdam: Board Publishers, 2009a.

Lucas, R. 'Designing Ambiances: Vocal Ikebana and Sensory Notation' in *Creating an Atmosphere Proceedings 2008*. Grenoble: CRESSON, 2009b. www.cresson.archi.fr/AMBIANCE2008-commSESSIONS.htm

Lucas, R. 'Gestural Artefacts: Notations of a Daruma Doll.' in Gunn, W (Ed.). 2009. *Fieldnotes and Sketchbooks: Challenging the Boundaries Between Descriptions and Processes of Describing*. Peter Lang Publishers, 2009c.

Lucas, R. 'Designing a Notation for the Senses' in *Architectural Theory Review Special Issue: Sensory Urbanism*, Spring 2009 Issue. Volume 14, Issue 2, p173. 2009d.

Lucas, R. 'The Instrumentality of Gibson's Medium as an Alternative to Space' in *CLCWeb Special Issue: Narrativity and the Perception/*

Conception of Landscape. Purdue University Press, 2012. http://docs.lib.purdue.edu/clcweb/vol14/iss3/5/.

Lucas, R. & Romice, O. 'Assessing the Multi-Sensory Qualities of Urban Space' in *Psyecology*, Volume 1, Issue 2, p263-276, 2010.

Lucas, R. 'The Sketchbook as Collection: a Phenomenology of Sketching' in Bartram, A., El-Bizri, N., Gittens, D. (Eds). *Recto-Verso: Redefining the Sketchbook*. Farnham: Ashgate, 2014.

Lucas, R.'Towards a Theoretical Basis for Anthropological People-Environment Studies.' in Edgerton, E., Thwaites, K., & Romice, O. (Eds). *Advances in People-Environment Studies: Human Experience in the Natural and Built Environment*. Göttingen: Hogrefe Publishing, 2014.

Lucas, R. *Filmic Architecture: an exploration of film language as a method for architectural criticism and design*. Unpublished MPhil by Research, Glasgow: University of Strathclyde, 2002.

Lynch, K. The Image of the City. Cambridge, Massachusetts: MIT Press, 1960.

Mauss, M. *The Gift*. London: Routledge, 2002[1954].

Meneley, A. & Young, D. (Eds). *Auto-ethnographies: The Anthropology of Academic Practices*. Broadview Press, 2005.

Merleau-Ponty, M. *The Phenomenology of Perception*. London: Routledge, 2002.

Miller, D. *The Comfort of Things*. London: Polity Press, 2009.

Miller, D. *Stuff*. Cambridge: Polity Press, 2010.

Moore, Thomas. *Utopia*. London: Penguin Classics, 2012 [1516],

Nesbitt, K. (Ed.). *Theorising a New Agenda for Architecture: Anthology of Architectural Theory 1965-95*. Princeton Architectural Press, 1996.

Orwell, G. *Why I Write*. London: Penguin, 1994.

Pardo, A., Redstone, E. & Campany, D. *Constructing Worlds: Photography and Architecture in the Modern World*. Prestel, 2014.

Pevsner, N. *An Outline of European Architecture*. London: Thames & Hudson, 2009.

Pevsner, N. *Visual Planning and the Picturesque*. Getty Research Institute, 2010.

Pickering, M. & Griffin, G. (Eds). *Research Methods for Cultural Studies*. Edinburgh: Edinburgh University Press, 2008.

Pike, K. (Ed.). Language in Relation to a Unified Theory of Structure of Human Behavior, The Hague: Mouton, 1967.

Pink, S. *Home Truths: Gender, Domestic Objects and Everyday Life*. Oxford: Berg, 2004.

Pink, S. *Doing Visual Ethnography*. Sage Publications, 2013.

Pink, S. *Doing Sensory Ethnography*. Sage Publications, 2015.

Redstone, E., Gadanho, P. & Bush, K. *Shooting Space: Architecture in Contemporary Photography*. London: Phaidon Press, 2014.

Reed-Danahay (Ed.). *Auto/Ethnography: Rewriting the Self and the Social*. Oxford: Berg, 1997.

Rendell, J., Borden, I., Kerr, J. & Pivaro, A. (Eds). *Strangely Familiar: Narratives of Architecture and the City*. London: Routledge, 1995.

Rendell, J. *The Pursuit of Pleasure: Gender, Space and Architecture in Regency London*. London: the Athlone Press, 2005.

Rkywert, J. *On Adam's House in Paradise*. Cambridge, Massachusetts: MIT Press, 1981.

Rkywert, J. *The Dancing Column: on Order in Architecture*. Cambridge, Massachusetts: MIT Press, 1998.

Rkywert, J. *The Judicious Eye: Architecture Against the Other Arts*. Cambridge, Massachusetts: MIT Press, 2008.

Rowe, C. & Koetter, F. *Collage City*. Cambridge, Massachusetts: MIT Press, 1978.

Rowe, C. *The Mathematics of the Ideal Villa and Other Essays*. Cambridge, Massachusetts: MIT Press, 1976.

Rykwert, J. *On Adam's House in Paradise*. Cambridge, Massachusetts: MIT Press, 1981.

Sadler, S. *The Situationist City*. Cambridge, Massachusetts: MIT Press, 1998.

Schlereth, T. J. *Material Culture: A Research Guide*. University Press of Kansas, 1986.

Schön, D. *The Reflective Practitioner: How Professionals Think in Action*. New York: Basic Books, 1984.

Sharr, A. *Heidegger for Architects*. London: Routledge, 2007.

Sharr, A. *Heidegger's Hut*. Cambridge, Massachusetts: MIT Press, 2006.

Shulz, A. *Architectural Photography: Composition, Capture, and Digital Image Processing*. Rocky Nook, 2012.

Sullivan, L. *The Tall Office Building Artistically Considered*. Getty Research Institute, 1896. https://archive.org/details/tallofficebuildi00sull (accessed 29/11/14),

Tafuri, M. *Interpreting the Renaissance: Princes, Cities, Architects*. New Haven, Connecticut: Yale University Press, 2006.

Tafuri, M. *Architecture and Utopia: Design and Capitalist Development*. Cambridge, Massachusetts: MIT Press, 1976.

Tafuri, M. *Theories and History of Architecture*. Cambridge, Massachusetts: MIT Press, 1981.

Tafuri, M. *Venice and the Renaissance*, Cambridge, Massachusetts: MIT Press, 1995.

Temple, N. & Bandyopadhyay, S. (Eds). *Thinking Practice: Reflections on Architectural Research and Building Work*. Black Dog Publishing, 2007.

Thwaites, K. & Simkins, I. *Experiential Landscape*. London: Routledge, 2006.

Thwaites, K., Porta, S., Romice, O. & Edgerton, E. (Eds). *Urban Sustainability Through Environmental Design: Approaches to Time-People-Place Responsive Urban Spaces*. London: Taylor & Francis, 2007.

Tschumi, B. *The Manhattan Transcripts*. London: Academy Editions, 1994.

Unwin, S. *Analysing Architecture*. London: Routledge, 2003.

van der Hoorne, M. *Indispensable Eyesores: an Anthropology of Undesired Buildings*. Berghahn Books, 2009.

Van Maanen, J. *Tale of the Field: on Writing Ethnography*. University of Chicago Press, 1988.

Venturi, R, Scott Brown, D & Izenour, S. *Learning From Las Vegas* (Revised Edition). Cambridge, Massachusetts: MIT Press, 1997 [1977].

Ward, K. *Researching the City: A Guide for Students*. Sage Publications, 2013.

Yaneva, A. *The Making of a Building: a Pragmatist Approach to Architecture*. Peter Lang Verlag, 2009.

Yaneva, A. *Made by the Office for Metropolitan Architecture: an Ethnography of Design*. Rotterdam: 010 Publishers, 2009.

Index

Figures in *italics* refer to illustrations.

Acknowledgments

This book includes material from a range of research projects and collaborations across my career so far. This research has been supported by a range of bodies including the Arts & Humanities Research Council (AHRC); Engineering & Physical Sciences Research Council (EPSRC), European Research Council (ERC), and University-based organizations such as the Manchester Institute for Research in Art & Design (MIRIAD at Manchester Metropolitan University) and institutional funds at the University of Manchester.

Early projects working with my mentor Per Kartvedt at the University of Strathclyde helped establish an agenda for my inquiries into architecture. This time also included working with a range of others including Jonathan Charley, Oren Lieberman and Gavin Renwick, to each of whom I owe a great deal. Tim Ingold, my PhD supervisor and mentor, introduced a degree of rigour to my thinking, and encouraged an appreciation of what fundamental activities define ourselves as human. This collaboration continues to this day, from the *Creativity and Practice Research Group,* where I was supported by group Wendy Gunn, Murdo MacDonald, Sandra MacNeil and Arthur Watson, and evolving to form the ERC Funded *Knowing from the Inside* project, where I consider myself lucky to work alongside a committed group including (but again not restricted to) Mike Anusas, Stephanie Bunn, Emilia Ferraro, Amanda Ravetz, Anne Douglas, Jen Clarke, Jo Lee Vergunst, Griet Scheldeman and Rachel Harkness; each have contributed a great deal to my approach to research.

Further research posts at the University of Edinburgh and University of Strathclyde are also represented here, and the aid of colleagues here was crucial to my work. Again, many others helped, but Richard Coyne, Peter Nelson, Martin Parker, Wolfgang Sonne, Ombretta Romice, Gordon Mair, Stephen Cairns and William Mackaness all deserve special thanks for helping me to cross disciplinary boundaries between architecture, music, sound design, digital design, geography, urban design, product design and more.

For the past six years, Manchester School of Architecture has been my academic home; firstly at Manchester Metropolitan University and then at the University of Manchester. Throughout, students in my *Graphic Anthropology, World Urbanism* and other classes and studios have helped enormously in shaping this book, by asking the right questions, looking for clarification, and engaging with their own research questions. Colleagues past and present who have assisted (often without knowledge of giving this help) include, but are not limited to: Tom Jefferies, Albena Yaneva, Colin Pugh, Eamonn Canniffe, Nick Dunn, Richard Brook, Becky Sobell, Amy Hanley, Rick Dargavel, Sally Stone, Darren Deane, David Brittain, David Haley and too many more to mention.

The faith shown in the project by Laurence King Publishing has been heartening throughout the process, and I cannot thank Philip Cooper, Liz Faber and Gaynor Sermon enough for their patience and straightforward approach in guiding me through the process of publication. Thanks also to my two interviewees for the final chapter, Robert Adam and Craig Dykers, who gave so generously of their time and wisdom.

The most important acknowledgments are for my family. My parents Sandra and Andrew Lucas supported me through my early career, often puzzling at the odd directions my work would take me in, putting up with a drawing board in the kitchen for years, and listening to me rehearsing arguments and thinking out loud. Without their understanding, support and sacrifices, I would not have been able to make a career in research. More recently, that support has come from my wonderful wife Morag, who has given patient advice when I run out of time, has put up with my pacing about and staring into the distance while I think about how to phrase something. Morag also provided invaluable assistance in preparing the section on archival research, being a professional archivist by trade.